Leaving Wayne

A story about overcoming trauma, poverty, and addiction while growing up in a time of radical change

DANNY CLUNE

iUniverse, Inc.
Bloomington

Leaving Wayne
A story about overcoming trauma, poverty, and addiction
while growing up in a time of radical change

Copyright © 2012 Danny Clune

iUniverse books may be ordered through booksellers or by contacting:

iUniverse
1663 Liberty Drive
Bloomington, IN 47403
www.iuniverse.com
1-800-Authors (1-800-288-4677)

ISBN: 978-1-4759-4901-8 (sc)
ISBN: 978-1-4759-4900-1 (hc)
ISBN: 978-1-4759-4902-5 (e)

Library of Congress Control Number: 2012916495

Printed in the United States of America

iUniverse rev. date: 10/5/2012

This book is dedicated to all my children
who let me grow up with them…
To all my recovering brothers and sisters throughout the world…
To Coon Hill Johnny, who took the long road home…

Illustrations and cover design by James Clune

Chapter 1

I think that the backseat I lay on belonged to a Buick—probably a '53—a smooth, rolled satin seat, brownish gray in color with a musky odor that smelled old but looked unworn. At that moment I couldn't have cared less, yet the surroundings were so vivid. What next caught my attention was the sky that was my favorite blue; it was the color of a clear autumn day, no wind and no clouds. Today I call it a September 11 day. There was brightness to the air that seemed unusual. My senses were hyped, I guess. I saw dust bunnies scrambling up the sunlight toward the back quarter window; there was a fly on the back of the driver's seat, and a buzzing sound that came from a competitor. It was bouncing around like only those half-dead flies can when the days get shorter. They dance to the sun and disappear into some dark crack for the rest of the winter.

I could hear voices that sounded troubled, although who was talking was not clear. They were near me—I could see four legs belonging to two men, but their voices were only pained sounds. What a beautiful day it might have been, except that I couldn't feel anything but a throbbing pain from the neck down. My body felt like it was one big wound. I tried to move, but I could not. My torso felt like it was unattached to my head, and my hands and fingers were lying useless, unable to respond to my wishes, even if I had any. They were bound to my sides by a mix of thick blood and hot, smelly oil. There were black and red splotches of goo splattered against the back of the front seats that had been part of me. They did not seem to have any pattern to them. I couldn't say that I was tossed there, but almost. I was wrapped in fiberglass insulation like a worm inside a cocoon, foil to the outside and the itchy part to the inside. What a strange way to travel!

Soon we were moving at breakneck speeds over an unsure road. The Buick smacked over a crack in the concrete highway, and I blacked out, only to come to and have it happen all over again and again. I finally gave out somewhere around Deposit, New York. As things faded rapidly I could hear the sound of Jack Brennan and my dad talking; they sounded afraid. I don't blame them. Had I been conscious, I would have been afraid too.

Sometime later, I awoke to a lady in white; I was tied to a gurney. It seemed like forever before anyone said anything to me. I was blinded by a bright white light that was overhead. I thought I smelled gasoline, it was ether, a vile and wretched stuff that I would rebel against many more times in the next year. I was in a white room, so shiny and clean, so starchy and crisp; the air seemed thick. Time had slowed way down; I felt dirty just lying there. Many things were going on in this place, and I heard the word *surgery*. I saw a corkscrew light spiraling downward, and another light shone right into each eye. Bright images of a black-and-white checkerboard appeared close to me and then far away. A strong hairy arm held a rag over my face, and by the time I thought about pushing it away, it was too late. There was total silence, but I was screaming … I think. A black-and-white hole sucked the noise, the light, and me down a tunnel where I didn't want to go. I wanted my daddy.

Chapter 2

BINGHAMTON, NEW YORK

THE "WARD"—IT WAS A STRANGE name for a room. To me, it was a long green room of iron-barred cots. There were strong-looking women dressed in starched white uniforms who seemed less than happy to see me. When they walked they sounded crispy. The room was large and had one way in; I couldn't find a way out.

The hard mattress in my cage was cream colored with blue stripes; others had pissed and shit on it before me. The mattress had a thin sheet that covered it, but the yellow and brown spots could be seen through the well-worn cotton. The women would turn it over from time to time, but the stains just changed places. The tall bars of the steel bed cast shadows across the dull room—crib bars that kept me contained. The paint was chipped; scars left from past kids. How long would this last? At seven you worry about these things. I saw someone's name half-scratched above my head, leaving the metal with a partial autograph that was not legible. Months later I would add my name.

I wanted to go home yet I knew that this would not end soon. There were long days where boredom was interrupted only by food. The meals were something to wait for at least. During the day there were people and noise—it was something. On Thursdays and Saturdays, a girl named Linda, who was in a wheelchair, would come and read. The rest of the week was lying in a cage imagining that you were not forgotten. There were longer dark nights that I shared with the bogeyman. I imagined that shadows were people. I gave them names, mr. and mrs. lonely. I got to know when they would arrive. I was always scared. No one spoke to me most days and less at night. No one came to see me, and no one cared where I was. Shots came frequently (there was always the lie about how it wouldn't hurt). My ass was a pincushion and my arms covered with welts, all in the name of getting better. You get used to the needles; you learn lack of trust from the lies.

The casts on my leg were thick, and they were changed monthly. The bandages were wrapped with chalky paste, sponged with water, and they hardened like masonry board. I smelled of rot, like the leaves that piled up wet in the fall. The more I sniffed, the worse I smelled. I could not stop testing the air for the odor even though it made me gag. I never knew what the attraction was. Maybe I was smelling myself to see if I was alive.

Each day was the same; through the window, the air looked as if it had turned brown, leaves fell, it snowed, and gloom arrived. Winter brought no new visitors. I was getting upset. It was then that I began to cry. My ward mates were Gary, who had a brown mop for hair, and Wayne, who was a redhead. They both were seven and did not talk much. They were in body casts, and each day got hoisted up to lay with their legs extended, on the rack. Wayne smelled worse than me, like dead skin. We all scratched ourselves raw. The trick to a good scratch was to keep a butter knife from dinner. At night you would push it down inside your cast and then wiggle the knife and push your leg against the iron bars. I invented the knife scratch, and we all did it.

Gary and Wayne were there two years. They did get time off for Christmas and got their casts changed before they went home. I got one year, no time off. We were the inhabitants of general hospital kids' ward #2. We were in a pediatric jail. Then there were the not-so-friendly visitors, including an orderly we called Mr. Oil Change. My memory of him is buried deep inside. Gary and Wayne would cry when he was on the ward, and I would get ready. It was a ten-minute mineral oil rub with hands and fingers that belonged someplace else and left me with bad thoughts. Oil stole my toys that I got for Christmas; model planes and ships that he said he would put together for me. I never saw my toys again. Fridays were phone calls from home, rarely for me. Long distance with party lines for four minutes, and sometimes not. There was less of me left when Friday night waned. It was this way for months. There was depression, deep and numbing; there was guilt and shame; and there was darkness. Who cared? I cried for my mommy and daddy, but no one listened.

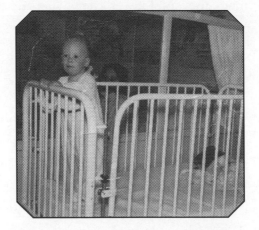

Chapter 3

Preston Park, Pennsylvania

Preston Park really doesn't exist; there is nothing of note that would tell you arrived there, no proof of a real name or a need for one. It was no place for historical markers. There once was a sign at the crossroads of PA 370 and 247, but the last time I looked, a few holes probably made by buckshot had ripped it up, making it look more like a sieve than a sign. If you take 191 S. from Hancock, New York, for one mile, turn right at Pete and Lovey's on Route 370, and head west for nine miles, you come to Archie Rooney's corners. Turn right at Porosky's sawmill. You're now in Preston Park.

Earlier in its non-history there was a schoolhouse on an old and abandoned road that went from behind the mill down to what was Russ and Winnie's store. My dad went to the school as a kid. George Walters built a house there. When George died, Viola, his wife, with kids to raise, moved away. Ronnie Mead bought the house after that, and he still lives there last I looked.

The road there from Preston Park to our house was curvy, and about a half mile up there is, or was, a railroad trestle on the left and a stone bridge on the right, where everyone dumped garbage and other unwanted items in the small creek underneath. We shot rats there. As you got closer to my house, things got more interesting. Mr. Mead was a mysterious man to us kids; he was stooped over and wore brown-and-gray pants with suspenders. He never spoke except to tell us "to git!" I was told he would drink anything that had alcohol in it. He also grew a lot of potatoes in a garden behind his house that he worked with his team of horses, these were kept in an old ramshackle barn. Neither he nor the horses were seen except at a distance in his potato field.

He once came to our house on a fall evening, demanding something to drink; he left with half a bottle of Castoria and most of a pint of rubbing alcohol. He had a rupture, and his gut hung low as he waddled up the road. One winter evening, just after dark, Dad dug him out of one of the deep snow banks that were piled along the roadside, put there by the snowplows that came by after a winter storm. Mrs. Mead was loving and kind. She would make fry doughnuts and save us all the holes—rolled in powdered sugar, they were a welcome treat.

When walking home on the road from the four corners, things started to play in your mind. Running didn't help, it only confirmed that something was hiding somewhere behind the many trees that lined the road home. One big obstacle was that you had to walk by Mr. Mead's barn to get home. I always hurried and closed my eyes as I passed. You could smell the horses and sometimes hear them in their stalls. I could imagine them running with their big shoes clanking behind me, although they never did. Another obstacle was the wooden bridge between the scary barn and our house. We were told as young children that trolls lived under it. There must have been a lot of creosote around in the 50's because it got slapped on everything, including the bridge. Stinky stuff and tar-like, it grabbed at your sneakers as if it was a trap that was set up to catch you as you passed. The railings on the bridge were rickety too. They creaked as we ran across them as if the faster we ran, the safer we would be. A train running under the bridge would shake the whole thing. If you were on the bridge when the train came, you were surely in danger.

My sister Betsy had a dog named Duke, a German shepherd that had light-brown fur. He was quite calm but would bite sometimes as if to let you know he could if necessary. He liked to chase the different men who came knocking door-to-door, selling things out of their paneled trucks. Vegetables and eggs and meat were delivered by truck, if you could call it that with its wooden sides and blocks of ice pretending to be refrigeration. Most of them came from a place called The Valley and a town named Carbondale. These places were all far away, yet I could picture the image of a valley in my mind. I wasn't sure about Carbondale. The name Carbondale did little to feed my imagination.

Up the hill from our house was the Homer Curtis farm. We bought milk from them for fifty cents a half gallon. It had lots of cream on the top that both Mom and Dad liked. Dad would put it in his coffee and then drink the coffee out of his saucer; Mom made butter from the rich yellow cream. Later on we got a cow and had our own milk. Homer was nice; he was tall and always neat and clean, even when he worked in the barn milking cows. Lauren, the oldest boy, treated us well; he let us help him with chores sometimes. We got on the school bus in front of their house, as the bus did not go past ours. Sandy, the oldest and only girl, always got on the school bus first. She was quiet and firm. I usually sat near her on the bus. The younger boys I didn't know until we grew older. Richard and Jeffrey were their names, but I rarely saw them. The family worked hard (they were Methodists). Once Lauren let me help him chop silage off the frozen walls of the silo that stood beside their barn. These were important chores for a farm boy. At one point I ran a pitchfork into my foot; it went right through my foot and into the sole of my boot. That incident ended my silage-chopping career.

One summer, a man named John Hunt came to dig us a cellar entrance to our house, as our furnace was broken and there was no way to get the old one out and the new one in. He had a digging bar and a shovel and a pick. I watched him dig all summer. I played in the pile of sand he used for cement and the dirt he dug up from the basement wall. He said little and drank from a silver-and-red thermos and sweated a lot. That was most of the excitement I had that summer. One time Jimmy, my older brother, and I went up on the big rocks hunting snakes. This was a great adventure. The snakes liked to lie out on the sunny side of the flat rocks that were abundant above our house in Curtis's pasture. We were brave cowboys who would attack the sleepy lumps of scales. We would leave them for the Indians that never showed up to get them. We had our favorite cowboys—I was Roy Rogers and Jimmy was the Lone Ranger. We wore our cap guns low and were fast on the draw, and we were undoubtedly the best cowboys in Preston Park.

Outside of our imagination, not much else ever happened there. Occasionally for more excitement than killing snakes, we used to play chicken with our bicycles. One of us would ride to the top of Curtis's hill and the other would park sideways on the bottom of the hill. One bike would fly down the hill, faster than you can imagine—sometimes faster than the other bike could get out of the way! You get the picture.

There was a rhubarb patch across the road. We would pick the red stalks and dip them in sugar for a summer treat; they were sweet and sour all at once. The best treat was the ice cube trays filled with Kool-Aid; we could put a stick in them and suck on the frozen flavored ice. I looked forward to the fall when I could go with my dad to his garage in Lakewood and clean tools and sweep out the school bus that he drove each morning and afternoon. That was where all the trouble started that launched me into the hospital.

Chapter 4

THE LAKEWOOD GARAGE

SATURDAYS WERE SPECIAL. THERE WAS no school and it was my turn to go to "the garage." The Lakewood garage was a concrete block bunker of a place where the walls sweated in the long summer and frosted in the longer winter, and that was on the inside. The garage was a post–World War II experiment in free enterprise for my dad. The Lakewood crew would roll in slowly; Saturday was half a day's work. Most were Dad's friends, and they knew each other as kids. Steve Simpson, my sister's godfather, was a short wiry guy with an attitude well earned from surviving the "death march" and the "Japs." He had been on Corregidor and lived to tell about it. Also, a few local men with more affection for each other than a regular job would provide gathered at noon and sat on tires and ate lunch from waxed paper wrappings. Some came to get tires changed or brakes fixed. Some just to bullshit. George Lewis worked for Dad at times. He talked funny, always looked scruffy, and was all muscle. I think he did what was called the dirty work. Dad paid him cash. He had little status among the older men, but you could tell they all loved him.

Benny C was there with his new Chevy (after the "accident," this would cause a conflict and resentment with my dad that existed for many years). Jack Brennan, a Brooklyn transplant and John Bircher to the bone was a loyal friend to Dad and would remain so forever. Jack would later work for Dad as a bartender; a likely pulpit to preach against the communist threat that Jack assured everyone was among us. The men took Jack with a grain of salt, but he could be convincing. Jack owned the Buick I mentioned earlier. Joe Wood may have dropped by, and certainly Al Evanitsky, too, before the morning was over. Gas, Mobil brand, was twenty-three cents a gallon. Mike Torrick might stop by; he limped and all the guys seemed to like him because he was rich with humor and made them laugh. If we were lucky, we would get to go to the local hotel for lunch. The Lakewood Hotel was owned and run by a leprechaun named Frank McGraw. Frank was salty in a friendly and endearing way, as his main objective was to gather gossip. The local guys would tease him about his thriftiness and embellish local stories for him to feed on.

I loved this gathering time, yet lunch never came this particular fall Saturday, except through a feeding tube, and I didn't get to share it with anyone in Lakewood, Pennsylvania.

The truth is that I was allowed to go to the garage with my dad because this was a way for Mom to get a break—with seven spawn, she needed it. My job was to sweep out the school bus that Dad drove each morning and evening through the hilly roads of Rock Lake, Pennsylvania. This part-time job provided some health insurance and cash money, something that was in short supply in the 1950s.

Long, lean, and mean was his bus. School-bus yellow. Chevrolet, straight six with a four-speed transmission and thirty-six seats—bus #37. Some seats ripped, some not, and halfway down, a worn rubber-matted aisle there was a heater on the left side. Someone had kicked the guard off. My job was sweeping out a week's worth of kid shit, my first job. Movie-theater-style garbage, sticky and stinky. I remember starting the cleanup and then wandering into the garage to eat lunch. But lunch didn't happen. *Boom* did! A flash, a rush of hot stinky air, pieces of an old truck, parts from an oil tank and some wood, and me—dizzy, falling, and flying. I heard fighting about cars, then blackness, then Benny and Dad, then angry words, and then Jack and Dad. Oil and blood and small pieces … of me. Later on, this all was made sense of for me, not ever by me. I wish I had been in the bus. Anyhow, that's how I got into the backseat of Jack Brennan's Buick, listening to a fly buzzing.

Chapter 5

RETURNING HOME

WHEN I CAME HOME FROM the hospital, I was not okay. I felt like something was missing—time, a big piece of my leg, and much skin off my ass. There was a disconnection with what had passed away in the last year. It was difficult seeing all my brothers and sister again. Mom seemed different; I hadn't seen her for several long months. I had gone away and everyone else kept on living—there seemed to be an unfairness to that. My world was somehow apart from theirs, and I couldn't plug in. I scooted around on a board with wheels or on crutches; lots of folks paid a visit but treated me as being different.

There was the guilt and shame. I had taken on the guilt of separating from my family and leaving them alone. I had the guilt of once again not being where I belonged in my family and in a sense what I was worth to my family. I felt that I had let my family down. Shame ripened later on when I saw how poor we were, and I heard my mom say that "if you hadn't been in the hospital" and "if you knew how much you cost." I always wondered about this abstract idea; how much did I cost?! As time went on and the family "fortunes" declined, my value went down too, apparently. I knew then that I was not normal—I was unhappy and not wanted. I saw things that others did not. I was hyper-vigilant, which is common for trauma victims.

School was no better. Second and third grade were all mixed up. I left in second and returned about halfway through third. Parents and teachers did their usual parental dog-and-pony show and labeled me bright enough to catch up. Catch up to who or how? Little did they know how little I knew. My brain didn't work well, and I could not hear out of my right ear. These were secrets. Somewhere I crossed a line and became angry and depressed. The probable brain damage was not noticed. The focus was on obedience and not talking unless you were asked. I had too much to talk about, and it came out sideways. But I was seven and didn't know what sideways was, and who gave a shit anyway? The safety of first grade and Mrs. Coveney's class, her hugs and loving patience, those childhood memories were gone. The sandbox and chocolate milk and recess and laughter. This is what I left abruptly, and what was quickly erased by third grade and Mrs. S. Warm to cold; safe to sorry; yum to yuck. The many thoughts of a child when change is forced upon him are powerful; mine led me to escape and survive.

The ruler ruled in Mrs. S's class. Write a hundred times that you talked out loud, bla bla bla. Don't talk! ... Don't talk? Are you kidding me? I just wanted someone to listen. My knuckles hurt from the ruler's edge cracking against my knuckles. The little strip of brass on the edge made small cuts and large wounds. I wanted to cry, but I would not. This biddy could do a quiet shuffle as she came up behind me. She would pace the room. A quick and well-positioned slap at the back of my head. Hair pulling. Ear grabbing. My head hurt, my hair hurt, and fifty years later, it all hurts.

Once during recess I was venting some choice marine phrases

aloud toward Roy R. His quiet and nice way made an easy target. I cursed out loud! I called names! The words were foul and hurtful. I knew I was wrong but had lost control of my anger. Had I lost all of myself? I do know that for that minute of rage I was not aware of what I was doing; the surroundings became quiet. I had found relief in madness.

Mrs. S had the response. She washed my mouth out with soap—Ivory I think. Seemed fair at the time to her. You could see the pleasure in her face as she stuffed the bar into my tightly clenched teeth. Finally she must have had enough and just stopped and walked away.

There were some nice things in third grade. Christine G., cute, sat in front of me, and my first crushes on girls were of her and another named Theresa B. And there was J. R. Evanitsky, the coolest guy in third grade. He sat next to me. Most of the class, especially the boys, had learned to keep their heads down and voices quiet. Some of us had fun, but it cost you dearly. My grades reflected my fun. Since no one cared about my grades, fun was the better choice. Fun was running around playing tag and teasing the girls into the cloak closet. This was all done at recess or when there was a substitute. It also gave me relief. I was spinning free, a child dervish.

But if things were difficult in third grade, hell was just around the corner. Somehow the decision for me to go to Lake Como School was made. With the prospect of facing the blue-haired Hun again, I opted to go to school there. The school was built around the time of the Civil War and had only been updated with electricity and a toilet as far as I could see. The old wooden building stood atop a hill with a dirt road that was barely passable, and that was in the summertime. Ruts and cinders seemed to make up the road, the remnants of last winter. Spring brought a torrent of water, summer was dusty, and winter brought ice. The fifth season was mud.

I saw my future through the eyes of an eight-year-old, but I wasn't blind. My fourth grade class had seven students, and as the newcomer I had little status. Everything inside the school was cleaned and varnished to begin the year. There was deep evidence that these desks were not new. Who was "FU"? It was scratched in large letters across the back of my attached seat. Mr. Baker was not unkind, just from an earlier century. He ruled with the paddle and a touch of shame; few words were spoken. Fear was alive in this one-room classroom. If any of the kids needed attention, well C. K. gave it to them. I was glad when that year was over. Fourth grade really sucked. I think of it as a flicked piece of dried snot, shooting across the room off the end of my finger. One year of my life then, a scar now. Seven was not a lucky number for me.

Chapter 6

THE FARM IN LAKE COMO

PART 1

I, AS MOST CHILDREN OF my era, had little say in family matters. We usually found out about changes that were happening within the family about one minute before they actually happened. Moving from Preston Park to the farm in Lake Como seemed like that, overnight and with little planning. One wonders what makes adults act the way they do.

Our house in Preston Park was crowded with one bath and four small bedrooms, and there were five boys and two girls who were reaching the age where more privacy was needed. Work also was needed to keep us all busy, and we were reminded how important that was by our mother. The refrain was always about how hard she and Dad worked to give us what we had—and they did. So it seemed to me that I went to bed in Preston Park and woke up at the farm in Lake Como. Quickly, I had gone from a boy to a young man with responsibility, yet emotionally I was still an infant. My time in the hospital, several surgeries, the loss of body parts, and any thoughts of further recovery, either physically or emotionally took second fiddle to the massive amount of change that rolled toward us like a storm. It would shake our whole family's underpinnings.

The outside of our farmhouse was a version of hard fiberglass pieces that were made to resemble painted shakes. Someone before us had painted them white, but the years had yellowed them in spots. It could have been whitewash and not paint, and it would have looked the same. Up the side of the house ran a wire that stuck through a window on the bottom floor. This was connected to the antenna on the roof that pointed north in order to get the one channel that was available. Soon we would have a TV to connect to the other end of the wire. This let us watch *Ed Sullivan*, *The Lawrence Welk Show*, and on Sundays the *Little White Church by the Side of the Road*.

It appeared that there were half storm windows from the outside of the house, but there was no evidence of them working, and the glass in some had been broken or cracked. On the inside, the slides were broken too.

The first room you entered was a long summer kitchen that still appears today in my dreams, with lift-up windows that were screened, and benches that came down from the walls to accompany a long table. I had never seen anything like this before, and we gloried during that first summer in using that room as it was intended for all meals. This was also the room where Mom insisted that our barn clothes go when entering the house, and we were glad to have barn clothes to take off, whatever they were—often, old coats and rubber boots well patched like old tire tubes, hats of several varieties, and gloves. Brown gloves! This was the stock in hand clothing for farm folks that could almost be worn on either hand, and were! When a mate had too many holes or went missing, you could wear one under the other to cover the worn-through areas that suffered the most. There was fierce competition for these items, and as four of us boys were within close age of the others, we invented many ways to hold on to our better items and pass off on our brethren the worst of the lot. Survival was one way to get your needs met.

I had a bluish-sheen coat with a hood that was trimmed in fur, probably some unlucky rabbit. I wore long johns under jeans that Mom had sewn patches on over worn knees. Rubber boots were stuffed with waxed paper when they became cut or the soles wore out. The tops could and often were patched like inner tubes, but the bottoms held little promise of repair. There were times when we got new ones, usually Christmas or a birthday. Money was tight and I knew that because it was often what Mom and Dad fought about.

There was a large storage room behind the summer kitchen, and this was the repository for all the junk that we were not ready to part with yet. Among the many items were lawn mowers and parts for old mowers long retired. Tools of various sizes and value and just about anything that a family of nine had no place to put ended up there. Later on this would be the go-to place to find anything that you were sent to find. Often without details, you would rummage through the piles with ever-building anxiety lest you came back to Dad empty-handed. It was a guessing game that you could not win.

The regular kitchen had a stove that took coal and gas—a eunuch, neither good with gas nor good with coal. What this stove was good for, except Mom's great cooking, was a place to dry your clothing at the end of the day and an oven to warm your feet in the morning after a night of frostbite during the long winter months. It also supplied ashes to throw onto the ice that formed on the path to the barn.

In the main kitchen there was a large porcelain sink with the proverbial window so you could look out over the lawn while washing dishes, and a table that was crowded, even with the formica leaf that completed the set, when nine were around it. The classic blue table and the monkey metal chairs were '50s but only six in number, and we dragged other dining room chairs and stools (and usually a highchair) as needed to gather round the table. Mom could cook any type of stew, gravy, or soup ever made. If she made stone soup, it would have tasted good. She was a true cook, and she rarely sat with us to eat. Her main desire was to feed all of us and then she would eat what was left. I wanted her to sit down with us, and it bothered me a lot that she would not. I inherited that trait; today I rattle the pots and am the kitchen controller and not a bad cook.

It was cold the first winter, very cold; ice would form on the inside of the windows and snow would gather in the sills. You could see your breath from sundown on. There were times that we had little heat, as gas and heating oil were in short supply even as cheaply as the supply was. The house stood on a hill where the wind blew across an open and barren field. You could see the wind blowing inside the house. The few curtains and shades, such as they were, did little to insulate, and it was common to have water pipes freeze. There were two winters that I remember where the snow was so deep that the road in front of our house was closed for the better part of a week. While it was an opportunity to play in the snow, and digging tunnels was fun for us kids and a reprieve from school, you had to come inside sometime to thaw out. The long winter took its toll on the family in general and was not a good time for small dairy farmers. Sometimes we had to "dump" our milk out because we could not get it to the creamery to sell it. Milk was the only thing that we had to sell.

We now had a large house with six bedrooms, two bathrooms, two staircases, and few furnishings. We looked at the space in wonderment but soon began the territorial wars that siblings have about space to supply their own needs. I think that at the time, I was not aware of poverty. Nine people in the family seemed normal, although in our family it seemed that we were not all connected—at least I felt that way—except by anger and the need to survive.

Our bedrooms were soon claimed, and we realized that we had some mattresses and a few dressers and chests, but we basically lacked the items that made our other house a home. Because our bedrooms lacked furniture generally, the gift of space made it seem even emptier. While Mom did her best to keep the house in shape, it seemed like a battle that couldn't be won in spite of Mom's endless work. The blankets that we had were thin and the few bottom sheets were thread worn. A pillow full of feathers would puff out a few pin feathers with every use, and there was really no way that I could see to replace them. Many mornings I awoke grumpy and sour as the result of bad dreams. I would rock myself to sleep. No one really cared how you felt, and most often the only feelings I saw were Mom crying and Dad raging. There was little in between to consider.

Having my own room, I was free to "rock" without anyone seeing me; a habit I learned in the hospital and brought home to quell my fears. My thoughts were scary and they would parade unannounced in my head. Noise and fear of my Dad's raging could start the parade too. I liked to be away from folks and rock myself to a state of peace and quiet. Having 160 acres, a large house, and a barn, I had many places to hide and find safety in.

I liked the barn in the winter because it was usually warmer than the house. Some thirty-five cows and a few calves and young stock can generate a lot of heat. I would go there and sit on the stairs to the haymow when no one was there between milking time. Somehow 3 p.m. was my best time and remains to this day. I self-adjust for daylight savings time.

The smell of cows is rarely offensive, unlike pigs or chickens which are the smaller animal on most farms. I would eat some orange pulp that had a decidedly breakfast aroma of fruit mixed with cereal. The cows loved this roughage, and I can say that at times I was grateful to share some with them. I was always hungry. I often ate some molasses-laden cow feed too; it had a sweet taste and filled me up. When it got below zero outside, the cats' milk would freeze like a white Popsicle in the old metal bowl we fed them in. Once it was fifteen below zero. Often, below zero went on for weeks.

As I sat in the barn, my mind would wander to things that were real and unreal. I would be at peace in a world undiscovered yet or often at battle where I ended up the hero; in the end, I would turn on the bad guys and win fame and fortune. As I got older, girls were in my mind—movies too. I spent many hours every day in fantasy and nobody would know (how could they?); conversations were usually with oneself. I would snuggle into some hay with the hot breath of the animals warming the air and pretend that I was someone else, somewhere else, and a peace would come over me. I would often nap at these times.

Chapter 7

THE FARM

PART 2

MORNINGS BEGAN WITH A JUMP-START by Dad, who was usually angry for the hell of it. There was plenty of hell, mostly directed toward Jimmy, who just could not get out of bed and to the barn on time (turns out he was nocturnal). Usually fifteen minutes was allowed before the hollering and cursing began. I was too scared and had a need to please, so I would get to the barn on time—usually 5:30. Sometimes I would run into Dad as he was heading back to the house to kick Jimmy's ass, and I gave him ample room as he raged up the path to the house. Dad could move; he was quick and could be on you before you said boo. The stress of poverty can trigger the deepest rage and unresolved issues, and Dad had plenty of both.

The main floor in the barn was bordered by gutters usually filled with cow shit, especially in the winter when the cows stayed inside. They could shit standing up, lying down, and probably other ways I had not seen yet! Later on we would get a barn cleaner (which isn't the proper term). It was a gutter cleaner, and when it worked it was a joyous thing, but when it didn't, shoveling between the paddles that pushed the manure out into the yard was twice as much work as it had ever been.

My job was one gutter and Jimmy had the other. Picture yourself standing in fresh cow shit up to your knees at 6 a.m.—at least the shit was warm. We had opted for a Patz barn cleaner, and it had paddles that were on a chain at intervals and would go around the gutters and push the shit eventually to a ramp outside of the barn and into a shit spreader or onto a pile when the spreader was broken or the weather was too cold to load it anywhere else. You could watch the manure head for the doggy door on its trip out and see it freeze by the time it hit the pile during the winter months. Naturally, anything that is mechanical can break down, but we thought that if we prayed to the Patz gods it would not break down. There are no Patz gods.

Such was the life: up at dawn, work in the barn, get cleaned up, and try to catch the 7:15 school bus that came on time. If you missed the bus, you could walk the three miles to the other bus stop at Archie Rooney's corners and be there at 8:15. If not, tough shit; get out the thumb.

After fighting your way through the bullies on the buses and being abused by teachers, fighting your way through the locker room on gym days and again back onto the bus, you headed home to chores. Chores usually were shoveling more cow shit, feeding the cows "cow feed" and hay, and then heading back to the house to eat and back to the barn for milking. Milking the thirty-some cows took about two or three hours, and pulling teats prepares you for little in life, except maybe accuracy with a squirt gun and an appreciation for breasts (the kind with one nipple). I could hit a running cat with a stream of warm milk at ten feet. I could also get my ass kicked if I got caught wasting milk. We had three Serge Brand milking machines that ran, but they were constantly being repaired because, frankly, many of our cows did not like a noisy suction device attached to them in such a sensitive place and would freely kick them off.

I don't believe that we really knew what we were doing as dairy farmers. Dad was raised in a different generation, Mom was from a city, and the seven kids were hardly big enough to lift their own weight. Jimmy was the oldest boy and expectations for him were high—impossible probably—and he rejected the whole concept of farming from as far back as I can remember. Betsy, the "parent child," was part of the house more than the barn and had her hands full as she was more of a parent than Mom was capable of. Cliff and Gerry were young, and Cathy and Mike were not of school age yet. Dad was a rage-aholic; Mom was emotionally disabled and deeply depressed. Cows just didn't like us, and every chance they had they showed it. The most effective way was by not giving milk, or little of it. We didn't exactly embrace the cow psyche, and Dad's rage had a detrimental effect on our sensitive bovines.

The upstairs, called the haymow, had a large bin where cow feed would be shoveled into a chute that traveled downward into a wheelbarrow and was doled out to each cow with a feed scoop— usually about two quarts per animal. We each had our favorite cows, and probably they got more than their share if no one was looking.

Cows are dumb; they have a limited capacity for developing prosocial habits and often miss the mark. Although they tried, they could not always find their particular stanchion when coming into the barn from outside. If one missed, the whole line simply adjusted until one brave animal would push back and the whole line repeated the jostle for a spot in the opposite way. Often you would have two heads wedged into one stanchion and would have to assist them in the rearrangement process. You may develop an attachment to a particular cow and like one more than another, but don't expect reciprocity. Sometimes cows would become deathly ill with "hardware" or break a leg or just quit; these poor souls were labeled as "downers" and shot. We would drag them down to the woods with the tractor, a chain around their necks. If you didn't go too fast, you could usually get that far before some part of the carcass gave loose. Usually it was Jim or me who had to do the dirty work. I think that we took turns; as obtuse as we were to trauma, these things stay chained down in the back of your mind forever. One of us would load the single shot 12-gauge shotgun or a 30-30 Savage rifle and shoot the animal behind the ear or through it. Cows died quickly, and this consoled me.

Every farm has its Abu Ghraib and we were no exception; there were few limits to our cruelty, not only to the animals but to each other. We had a cat named Tina and she could whack out three litters a year. She was tricolored, a very pretty cat and somewhat friendly for a barn cat. Tina aged and became almost blind. Over a period of a month, I watched her try to find something to eat, and she would bang into walls and soon developed a large sore on her head. We decided that it was more humane to kill her than let her live like this; however, killing a cat, even a blind one, is a lot harder than you think, especially when you are about ten or eleven years old. Anyway, I got Tina into a used burlap feed sack, no easy chore on its own. Because I really liked Tina, I decided that I could only stomach shooting her in the sack because then I could not see her. Somewhere things went awry and I half missed but managed to shoot the bag in half. Tina came crawling out, and blind or not, she had on her face a large question mark asking why I had done this to her. I tried to avoid any future assassinations of animals after that, and thankfully she died soon with the help of a solid whack over the head. These are the everyday abnormal lives of kids everywhere. I had a justification for my actions; it was expected and part of being "responsible."

Jim and I had different arrangements to vent our anger at each other. We tried to trick each other into various situations that gave us power over the other. Jim took the most physical abuse from Dad and others; I suffered the secondary trauma of those events because I witnessed them. Sometimes I think that not having the experience directly can have as deep an impact. More on that later.

Like most country kids, Jimmy and I welcomed the rite of passage that is called "hunting season." At about twelve years of age you could go hunting, and if you were lucky—or a consummate liar—you could have bragging rights about how big the deer you shot was. Most of the kids I knew inherited this trait from their fathers. Bucks counted more than does; misogyny exists in the existential world of our conquests. The more horns and the size of the horns were very important, and lesser racks were ignored or played down. To determine the accuracy of all the stories told by adolescent hunters, you would divide by eight and still have some falsehoods remaining. Jim and I now had our own guns. He had a 30-30 Savage with a bolt action and I had a Mossberg .410 shotgun with a clip and a bolt. Deer average about 150 pounds on the hoof, and either gun in skilled hands was adequate for the kill.

One off-season, Jim and I decided to hunt each other. I don't think we were angry at each other then; it was just where our imaginations took us. We chose Patton's swamp as the battlefield and had some ground rules. It was much like today's paintball, but when the players were "successful," there was a higher kill average. I remember that we decided that he had the more powerful gun and it was accurate at a greater distance, and I with the .410 should have more shells to even the competition. So off we went on the count of 120 away from each other, and the contest could then begin. Patton's swamp was mostly peat moss and bushes of wild huckleberries with some hard maple, ash, oak, and cherry trees of small-to-medium girth. In other words, "get down." About the first shot to the tree above my head, I shit my pants, but as a good soldier of fortune, I let three rounds go his way. Being out of ammo, I ran home to change my underwear. I must have been twelve years old. Jim and I never mentioned that adventure again until recently, and our versions still contain a fraction of macho.

Chapter 8

The Farm

Part 3

EVERY FARM HAS ITS OWN personality, and ours was a wild thing on a back red shale road. Lots of mud in the wet weather and dust in the dry weather; you cannot conquer red shale. This road separated the barn from the house and other buildings, and was our main thoroughfare. The house, the barn, and a collage of equipment sheds in back of the house all could have used some sprucing up, especially the "back sheds." The weathered boards shown through the many attempts of someone to slap some red paint on them, but without any serious attempt to make the place the farm of the month by any means.

Changes came radically with the seasons. All arrivals were harsh, although welcome, as the benefit of living in such a remote area was the ability to say good-bye to the last stretch of weather and welcome the possibilities of a newer season. The haymow would be barren by early summer, and the floorboards were rubbed shiny by the hundreds of hay bales that had been dragged over them the previous year. The smell up there in the mow would change too. When the mow was full by the end of the summer, it smelled as fresh as any new-cut lawn. The air would become humid and carry in it scents of the different grasses that were in each bale. Timothy, tree-foil, and clover were all there. There was a small chorus of smells all playing together if you breathed deep enough and inhaled carefully.

In between the seasons, the large areas where the hay was stored would vary in appearance and function. Building tunnels with hay bales and small "bale houses" at the end of each was an act of creation. We were simply children with lots of energy and little stimulation to balance what we desired to give. Of course in winter when it was too barren outside, the haymow was well insulated and a buffer from the weather—after all, the wind could blow you over and often did if you ventured too far from a shelter.

Inside my own hideaway there was a peace and solitude that would come over me; I was safe. You could measure the almost silence against the natural sounds of the wind groaning, as it worked against the weathered boards and steel roof. You knew it was brutal out there, but familiar. Hunkering down, I could have hibernated this way, as the cold has always made me sleep. In these quiet moments, maybe in a stupor, I struggled with the feelings of being different than other kids. I harbored a feeling of loneliness that had no logical explanation and that I did not see in others. My concern was that the next years before high school would expose me. I felt stupid—I couldn't understand math problems, and my thoughts were jumbled. Along with that I was sad and cried a lot—thick skin and thin emotions. I kept these things secret as much as I could and joined my family in denial of what oil explosions can do to the brains of young children. The family simply fled from the scene of the accident; I followed.

Earlier in the fall, you were closer to the roof of the barn as the hay was stacked high. It was exciting to look through the shrunken wall boards and be so far up in the air and still be safe from falling. You could see outside and no one could see you. I have always been excited by this advantage and had many places around the whole farm that I could see someone who could not see me. In the end though, there was nowhere else to go, so why not make your own place? I was a spy. I had discovered that my brother had also found the privacy of the warrens throughout the mows, and I was happy to find some racy magazines that had been hidden between the bales. He always could come up with important items at the right time, and I never told him that I, too, was interested in these fancy ladies with large breasts and a hint of nakedness that I found inside the pages. Coming up on fifth grade, these images excited me; my thoughts and body wandered and went places that I had not experienced before.

The haymow also provided us with our first gymnasium. We had two old vegetable baskets that we cut the bottom out of and nailed high up on the ending overhangs where you drove into the haymow. This area was usually half empty, and we swept the boards clear of hay and chaff. Any homemade ball (and the occasional real rubber ball) was used to play our various versions of basketball. We could play catch there too. Usually we had a stash of old baseballs and softballs that were found when we cut grass for hay or oats for silage in the field that neighbored Camp Wayne and their baseball fields. Seems that the kids would hit the balls into our field and leave them: finders keepers!

In all ways, grass was the beginning of a cash crop; without it there was no hay and no milk and no money. It was important that it grew abundantly, and we liberally spread cow manure on the ground throughout the winter and early springtime, knowing that the grass would reappear as sure as daylight came each day. I loved the way the grass pushed the snow and ice away come spring and could not be ignored. There was some natural trigger that alerted everything to the coming change, and soon the young shoots would confirm that. By late spring and early summer, the grass owned everything and needed to be cut or mowed. It was thick, with a depth of green color unmatched by any other means.

I would lie in the middle of a field, chewing on the butt piece of some timothy, and would get lost in the green of the grass and the blue of the sky. While there I could again quiet a troubled mind. A wren or sparrow would land on a piece of grass and, like a trapeze artist, would balance with the rhythm of the breeze against the thin stalk of growth. I wanted to be as free and as independent. This was a favorite place to while away warm late spring and early summer hours between chores.

We had lots of field and not too much pasture, so I had choices—a young person's fantasies need plenty of room to roam. I continued to be estranged emotionally during these days and spent many hours building forts in the woods, a tree house in the butternut tree that bordered the pasture and the road, and tunnels in the haymow where I could hide. The bogeyman was hooked in the back of my mind, and I still could not shake it.

We planted corn and oats with a rotation of crops that made sense to us. Newly turned fields seemed to grow rocks. They had to be picked out of the dirt before any planting could be done. You picked them up and put them on a stone boat as a tractor pulled the huge sled across the clumps of ground. Either you kept pace with the tractor or not, and then had to run to catch up with it, often to add your stone to the pile. When the boat was full, it would be dragged to the edge of the field and you threw the rocks off. Some of the bigger ones we would roll off the side of the stone boat, as they were heavier than us. Oddly I liked this work and always sought out wherever Dad was plowing to do it. When I was older and could be trusted to do this chore alone, I would put the tractor in low gear and give it just enough gas to not stall. With the steering wheel tied so the front wheels kept straight, I could walk behind the tractor and beside the stone boat. This allowed me to work alone, which was how I preferred it.

The first crop in any field that was newly plowed was corn. This is the main substance that went into the silo, and after sitting and fermenting it becomes silage. It was thoughtful to name something after its container. The silo, like the haymow, would be full in late summer and early fall. It was the tallest structure on many farms and ours was no exception; made of concrete blocks and ringed with steel binders, it resembled a huge barrel. There was a second silo next to this one; however that one was older, made of wood, and was falling down. We would often strip the boards off of it to build other needed pens and repair outbuildings.

The silage was layered in a natural order of harvesting. We would cut oats first and "blow" them into the top of the silo where they would fall to the bottom randomly. The tractor that powered the whole operation had a flywheel on its side, and a large belt about twenty feet long and a foot wide ran from the tractor to a wheel on a blower that was fed new-cut oats or corn or grass, depending upon whether it was from a truck or wagon, onto a conveyor. This was quite an operation, and with the tractor motor running at a high speed to supply enough power to the blower belt when a truck and or a wagon was unloading, any one thing could go wrong. Couple that with a truck engine and the noise of the oats blowing up the chute, and if something did break, it was easier to hear the change of noise than to talk to anyone.

The next crop would be the corn, and corn was heavy even though it had been chopped up. The solution was to have someone, Jim or me or both of us, in the silo to rake down the corn pile that accumulated there to even out the silage. This was tricky. Imagine being in a cylinder about twelve feet across and having corn blown down on top of you as you quickly raked down the pile and spread it evenly around. The best tool for this was a potato hook with three or four prongs that were sharp from hitting against the inside wall of the silo. What happens when corn with oats underneath begins to sit? They ferment. In the silo, where you are at the mercy of blowing corn or flying potato hooks, the air inside could easily intoxicate you. Maybe that was why we liked working in there. Our first drunk!

Chapter 9

The Farm

Part 4

EVEN THE MOST REMOTE FARMS have neighbors, and our farm had several, depending on which direction you went. We had Camp Wayne on one side and the old Patton Farm on the other side. Both of these neighbors inspired questions about who came and went in either place. Mostly the camp was deserted three seasons a year except for the caretaker, Russell Roney, a kind and generous neighbor. Exploration came natural to me, as it seems that most kids are curious. To me it was essential to know everyone and everything that went on around me. I was vigilant; a trait I had learned quickly while in the hospital. I could see the Patton house and barn, and the Camp Wayne for Boys ball field from our house.

The red shale road out front was passable most of the year, even by car. As kids, we walked. While this used up most of our leisure time the farm would allow, the journeys were mostly worth it. Social isolation is not the best environment for children to be raised in, and we pulled against the harness as often as we could as kids. Any traffic that went by was noticed and mentally recorded; the telephone, a six-party line, had an unwritten rule that you could listen in to others' conversations until someone would say "get off the line." There wasn't much being said that was enlightening, but it gives you some idea of how starved we were for other human contact. Listening to Hazel and some other biddy was only good for a later laugh and usually a giggle or two before we were noticed.

One uneventful day, I noticed an old car in the drive of the Patton place and smoke coming from the chimney. We thought that the place had been abandoned, and several sneak peeks through the windows had pretty much confirmed that no one had lived there for a long time. The place needed paint and the barn was falling down. The fields were mowed for the hay by the next farm up the road, owned by the Hempstead family. Because I was about ten and pubescent, I probably had more testosterone and less intellect than I needed, but I just had to know who or what was now living in the Patton farmhouse.

One day, on a bet, I rode my bicycle up there and knocked on the door. As a good citizen, I was going to welcome someone to the neighborhood. Bill and Marie both answered the door at the same time. They turned out to be quite a pair. Thrown together by some self-invented definition of domestic partnership, financial insecurity, Genesee Beer, and Pall Mall cigarettes, they seemed genuinely happy to greet this bold youngster who was starved for any contact with the outside world and had knocked on the door with assurance.

I looked up at a tall middle-aged man with Coke bottle glasses and yellow teeth. Next to him and closely aligned as her shoulder touched a little above his waist, was a same-aged female with unwashed hair. Somewhat troll-like in appearance, she seemed to be missing a neck. Behind them rolled out clouds of smoke that could have only come from someone smoking lots of cigarettes with little ventilation. In unison they said "hi" and "come on in."

The setting was simple: four chairs, one table, and painted wooden doors, mostly shut to any other space that I could see. A fire was going in the stove, and a space heater, probably gas fired, was near the rear side of the room where a dirty window and some raglike curtains kept any interested prying eyes out and some buzzing insects in. Below the window was a large porcelain sink that gave the indication that someone had eaten here within the past few hours—maybe only the dog, as a can of Alpo sat on the sideboard. I ventured in with all the bravery of an adolescent seeking new friends and willing to put first impressions aside. My entrance was greeted by the odor of cat piss and the unwanted affection of an aged and drooling dirty dog that appeared to have glaucoma.

In spite of my ignorance and need to roam, I knew that I had found a place that my house was superior to. The poverty and the dirt of this home was no match for my Mom's obsession with cleanliness. I could easily see that these were not folks who were interested in wasting time cleaning. After all, it would interfere with their card game and supportive habits. The game they favored and that my knock had interrupted was called "horse and pepper" and was played with a third "dead hand" as they were the only folks there and the animals seemed disinterested (except to rub against one's legs). I now know that Bill and Marie had other motives for welcoming me in—so their three-handed card game could have more validity.

I knew about cigarettes, as Mom and Dad both smoked, and Jim and I had toked on a few homemade butts of corn silk tightly rolled in toilet paper. What came as a great surprise was being ushered to a seat across from Marie and offered a Genesee and a

Pall Mall. Clearly these folks were not parents. I declined the beer that time, noting that a supply was close at hand, and pretended to smoke the long unfiltered roll of tobacco that Marie ironically labeled as "coffin nails." "Let the game begin," declared Bill, and it did. After about an hour, I excused myself for two reasons. One, I had to get home for chores, and two I had to go to the bathroom. I was uncertain about the indoor commode, even if there was any. As I pedaled away, hoping the smell of smoke on my clothes would fly off if I pedaled faster, I felt smug, knowing that I now had more knowledge than anyone else in my family about the goings on at our nearest neighbor. I couldn't wait to tell Jim. My first high was knowing something that no one else knew and feeling special—an important moment in an unrecognized world of lost youth.

It turned out that Bill soon stopped by our barn one evening while we were milking. He said hello to me and inquired of my dad about work in the area. My dad pointed him to the local camps, and Bill did find work at Camp High Lake. Bill also claimed to be an electrician and could see the sorry shape of our barn's energy distribution grid. There was some vague talk of appreciation on Bill's part and an offer to help do some rewiring. This of course was tacit approval for me to go visit their house at will. I would take Jim with me next time. I often longed for my older brother, however, early on learned he was on his own path, somewhat different than mine. We visited Bill and Marie several times and never caught them doing anything but playing cards, smoking, and drinking Genesee Beer. Soon we were smoking too, with a solemn oath that no one would tell our mom or dad.

One morning in the summer, Dad and I were walking together from the house to the barn when we both saw something hanging from a tree in the driveway of the Patton Farm. It looked like one of those Halloween dummies that you would hang from a tree to look like a ghost or a ghoul—only it was not Halloween. I could see the alarm in Dad's face. I had seen this look before when I was younger and had oil and blood on my face. Whatever it was, it was dangling there in the morning breeze and got Dad's attention. We hopped in the milk truck and he gunned our Chevy up there in a hurry. Sure enough, Bill had hung himself.

The lucky thing is that Bill had chosen an apple tree branch to throw the rope around. The branches of the apple tree were quite pliant, and as Bill had jumped off a large piece of wood that stood on end and was used for splitting firewood, the branch bent and his feet would touch the ground. He seemed uncomfortable but not dead or dying yet. Dad quickly cut the rope and Bill was free. My dad seemed visibly upset, more so than Bill, who looked up off the ground through his Coke bottle glasses that had miraculously stayed on (crooked but on), shook his head, and said, "Thanks Cliff, that hurt like hell." Domestic disputes had simpler solutions I imagined, and Dad and I didn't talk too much about it. There was relief, it seemed, in having neighbors who were crazier than us; we now had some normal status.

If you left the house by the back door and walked down the tractor path past the back sheds that served little purpose but held lots of promises and secrets, you quickly came to another smaller road that intersected with the main one that went past our house. This would be the preferred path to the school bus if you missed the 7:15 out front. This road followed our largest field until it came to the woods. This marked the property line for Camp Wayne (for girls). The road continued past what was the camp dump and ran down in the draw that was the homestead of the Coddington farm. One other house of note was on that road just prior to the intersection of PA 247, and that was where Billy Owens lived. Billy was my age and grade level. I knew that his mother smoked menthol cigarettes, because he used to clip them from her and share them with me. He had two sisters; one, Judy, had a physical disability. His father worked for Penn-Electric. After his other sister, who's name was Joy, lost her boyfriend to an unexplained drowning in their pond, they moved away.

The camp dump was a favorite place for us kids to rummage, especially after the summer was over and some great items such as good sneakers, an occasional baseball bat with a repairable crack, and an odd assortment of clothing that kids from the city lost or left behind. I think that the guys who worked at the camp as maintenance men got first dibs, and we got the leftovers. Jim and I would race to the dump after the camp truck went by, trying to be the first one to find that one unique item. We were prospectors, with the delusion that the next truckload would bring treasures—it rarely did.

Late in the summer, the local Catholic church, St. Juliana's parish, under the strict guidance of Father Merkel held their annual church picnic called "old home day." This was always held at the church in Lake Como. I ran the game where you tossed rings around a live duck's neck and got a prize or a duck. Most folks did not care for the large, fat white ducks or any ducks for that matter, as they shit everywhere if not penned. At the close of the day there were six left, and they were given to me for my labor. I had little orientation of how to care for ducks. Ducks are defenseless and somewhat unfortunate creatures that could be killed by some predator higher up the food chain; so I put them in a pen. Unfortunately for the ducks, the back shed was always under repair and the roof leaked like a sieve. That fall was cold, and when it rained, the water froze around the ducks' feet. When I went to check on them, they were as dead as ducks could be—sad but true. When the next year came around to the church picnic, I declined the duck ring game but never said why.

As third child, I inherited the characteristics of the marriage contract between my parents. Their constant fighting manifested itself as confusion for me. I felt obligated to stop the conflict but was too fearful to intervene. The trauma I felt seemed to overlay our whole existence. Our vegetable gardens died or were consumed by weeds, if they were ever planted on time. One evening Dad shot two deer, out of season, while arching across the fender of our milk truck. He smiled as he killed both with two shots. I went with him to gut them out and was told to leave them till next morning when he would take the tractor and the manure spreader (as a decoy) and drag the deer up to and hang them up in—you guessed it—the back shed. They rotted there as they hung till spring, and the rats ate from them.

There was one place back near the sheds where I sought refuge. Dad either bought or was given a Buick, '56 or '57 Century with an automatic transmission. Before very long the transmission went, and rather than fix it, we dragged it back by the sheds and put it on the list for future repairs. This was my secret hiding place. From about ten years old on, I had a novel stuffed under the front seat. Who the book was written by and what is was about I can't remember. I found it at the camp dump. What does remain clear as a bell is that if I could sneak out to the Buick and thumb the pages to a few salacious sentences that I imagined were about "love," I could get stimulated and masturbate. Usually I would take a nap, especially if the sun was shining, curled up like a cat, having reduced my anxiety naturally.

I thought my family was normal, though I discovered in the next couple of years this was not the case when it was compared to other families. There were many times that I wished I were someone else and prayed for that to be. My close friend was Billy, and he lived about three miles away, an easy walk made easier by our desire to smoke and his ability to steal cigarettes from his mom. These were the newer kind with filters and menthol. I was beginning to lie about most things I was doing if someone asked. No one at home usually did unless you got into trouble and they found out by hearing about it from someone else, usually a brother or my big sister. I took advantage of my mom's ignorance and easily stole cigarettes from her. She had recently switched to the filter brand, Winston, from the unfiltered Pall Mall for health concerns.

So Billy and I were bonded over nicotine and our interest in all things sexual. We both had sisters, and our older ones dated. This led to all kinds of supposition on our parts about intimacy, but we mostly got any factual (sic) info from magazines and off bathroom walls, and we communicated back and forth in school with notes. In fifth grade, we both had crushes on our teacher, Mrs. James, who was pregnant. This gave way to many conversations about how that happened and "how to do it." The only health education we received was from the school nurse, and that was about "Mr. Tooth," whose picture was on the wall in the nurse's office. He instructed us to brush up and down for fewer cavities.

Rather than focus on this important information, we passed notes in class. As luck would have it, between Billy and me sat Emily, with gorgeous blond hair and a developing bust line. It never dawned on me that Emily would have an interest in all this, but it seems that she knew a lot more factual information about sex than Billy or me. One of us drew a stick figure of a guy and a girl, and it got filled in by one of us with the word *fuck* attached to the note. Mind you, I am not condemning anyone, but the note ended up in my jacket pocket and life went on, almost. Life almost ended when I came home from school and my mother emptied my pockets and with tears in her eyes and moaning that she knew I was a "good boy," beat me silly with a metal dustpan. Such contradictions often led me to feel shamed and afraid of my body and its responses to sexual stimulus. Such was life, and although

I blamed the whole thing on Billy, I felt sick to my stomach for several days.

I began to have some troubling thoughts and behaviors during this time. Much centered on my growing interest in matters sexual and the need to keep these thoughts to myself. Several people including Sister Mary from religious education; Father Merkel, our priest; and now my mom all confirmed that these were dirty and impure thoughts. The beating Mom gave me solidified this philosophy. Now mind you, I didn't quite know what puberty was or what was happening, but there was a strange mixture of anger and a need to explode coming together inside of me. I watched cows give birth, even assisted in the process, and saw bulls mount cows and could understand that process, but it never was clear about humans and procreation. The many places I had created around our farm became my personal space and learning to masturbate was complicated. Being Catholics, of sort, we had it drilled into us that your body was a temple … but touching yourself or looking at yourself or sharing yourself with anyone else was a sin of the greatest magnitude. My only comment is that there were seven kids in our family.

Chapter 10

The Farm

Part 5

IT WAS IN THIS NEXT year that I developed an oppositional and defiant disorder toward the world. In other words, I "started the fire." The embers of this process had ignited many years before. I recall one day when change had occurred; however, to say that this was the only thing that was responsible for my rebellion would be an exaggeration. I was splitting, slowly but surely, and the tracks of my life were no longer parallel.

We were putting in hay, which means cutting, windrow raking, drying, and baling. Then the hay was stacked onto the wagon as high as was safe, usually four rows high, and taken to the barn to be put into the mow with an elevator. The smaller Ford tractor pulled hard to accomplish this task as the John Deere tractor kept baling in the field. This routine would not end until all the hay was successfully in the barn, about a month away.

It was hot. The sun beat down ten hours of the day, and there was no such thing as sunscreen, no shade, and no hats. We became like scalded meat—deep red. For relief at the end of the day, we would sit in vinegar baths to reduce the blistering. Eventually we browned, only to turn white again the next winter. The bales weighed sixty-five pounds, and we struggled to get them up onto the wagon where another person or two would stack them. I weighed about seventy pounds at this time. We had taken a break, and I sat under the wagon. Jimmy and Dan S. were shooting off their mouths as they stacked the hay bales I had loaded up to them, and I just wanted some quiet space. It was cooler down there out of the sun, and the wheels of the wagon made a good backrest.

Someone ran down to the milk house and came back with some cans of beer. I remember a green can and the smell of it as they handed some down to me under the wagon. "Ballantine Ale" read the label on the can and without hesitation I drank. The ale was cold, bubbly, and probably the foulest tasting stuff I had ever drunk, but there and then, sweating and thirsty, I took my first real drink of alcohol. It would not be my last for twenty-five years. I quickly finished the can and handed it back up to the older guys, yet something must have stuck with me, perhaps some flash of brief relief from all the feelings I felt and could not express. Who knows where folks keep their deepest thoughts.

Another sign of my "leaving the reservation" was that my body had started to reject the farm physically. I had somewhat forgotten that I was born with acute eczema and had spent some time in the hospital after being born and then again when I was about eighteen months old being treated for the skin lesions and the ensuing infections.

My skin had begun to exhibit what are generally called contact allergies, and huge blisters formed on the palms of my hands. In addition, the backs of my knees began to crack open. Anywhere I had a crease in my skin seemed to bloom into a painful infection that oozed pus. Now mind you, this could have been leprosy, but the amount of medical care that we received was on par with the cows, or not even. Actually, the most relief came from using bag balm, a yellow salve that was used to heal sores on the cow's milk bags and for other surface wounds, and keeping my hands covered with clean bandages. This doesn't work well for young boys keyed in on exploration of their environment and even more so, those responsible for farm chores.

Not that there wasn't concern. Mom did try to provide clean bandages and clean white socks to put on my hands at night, both to protect the wounds but also to protect myself from the scratching and digging I did to myself at night while sleeping. One wonders what really causes allergies, but stress could not be ruled out. Mom said that I was allergic to her milk at birth, yet I cannot find any medical evidence to support this. We simply never bonded; I was number three, that's all.

Financial problems became more acute for our family, as seven kids are a nine-person family at best with extraordinary needs. Total lack of food did not seem to be a problem, yet there was no extra; each meal disappeared quickly. My mother could cook the laundry and make a soup out of it that was tasty, but I believe that she often went without eating more than some leftover scraps for herself. There was no money—a dime or a quarter was coveted, and a dollar was unheard of. Arguments and resentments abounded throughout the house and spread to the barn, and I believe that my medical problems responded in kind. Birthdays and holidays were celebrated the best we could. Usually we got some item of clothing as a present, and that was fine with us as we always needed something.

I began smoking anything I could get my hands on—old butts taken from the milk truck ashtray, whole cigarettes stolen from packs left around, hay wrapped in cellophane, or corn silk wrapped in toilet paper. Young lungs could always get a puff or two from anything that would burn. You would be surprised at what you can get a buzz from.

Sixth grade went by quickly and was uneventful as our teacher stayed home with her first child and we had a "substitute" teacher. She was nice enough but no looker like Mrs. James, so we all suffered through the year thinking about girls and playing intramural basketball. I remember that I was not good at sports, even compared to the competition at Lakewood School, which probably wasn't much. I was always chosen last and often just given to the other team. There was not much esteem building that year.

Winter rolled in quickly that October and we had tons of snow. The cold weather also brought depression, another sign that something not good was happening. My sleeping pattern was abnormal, and I often felt like nodding in most of my classes, especially in the afternoon. My thinking conjured strange rationales for my disconsolation; by judging everything and everyone, I comforted my sense of self. Judging someone as less than or more than me gave me a place to belong. This comparing myself to others gave me self-satisfaction, and I felt in control. Actually I was afraid—scared of my thoughts, scared that I was not normal, scared that others knew this. Was this the beginning of living in fear or was this feeling there all along? As the long nights and short days of that winter rolled into spring, I had some realizations. These moods would be part of my personality for a long time, and I would tend to them.

The next year meant more changes, and there was some deal made with the local Preston School that allowed some kids to attend Hancock Central High School earlier than the normal ninth grade year. This meant riding two separate buses for me; the first one was on time and orderly. Elmer Hunt took no shit from anyone and would simply throw you off the bus if you did not behave. He also kept his bus clean and neat, so you always took your garbage with you. I liked this bus; it was safe. The second bus took high school students to Hancock from Lakewood and was named "the big yellow dick." This was not a safe place for us younger middle school kids.

Lack of safety simply meant the younger kids, like me, were going to get punched, pinched, titty-twisted, and ball broken for about ten miles before we could escape to our classrooms. If there were no seats up front—and there were usually none because good students and girls usually occupied the front seats—you ran the gauntlet to the back of the bus and took your hazing. I think that if I had fought back and just clocked one of those guys, it would have stopped, but I didn't. I was not a fighter except in my head, and many minutes were passed in mentally planning my attack on the bullies. None of these thoughts were pretty, however; they were fantasies. Coming home meant the same treatment all over again, except that some students stayed after school for sports, which meant that some of the jerks weren't there to torment us younger kids.

At home I started to hide away from the rest of my brothers unless it was mealtime or I had to be in the barn with them. I liked walking long distances alone to Lake Como or over the hill and through the pastures to see where this would take me. Usually I could find something new and unique to me. Seeing wildlife in their natural surroundings amazed me, and I particularly liked birds. I dreamed of flying away.

We were supposed to be Catholics, and this would usually mean catechism class or religious education during the week and church on Sundays. Catholics had their own printing presses, but the Bible, oddly enough, was not part of our religious education. My parents rarely went to church. I decided that saying I was going to church got me out of Sunday chores, and I usually headed down to Lake Como, just down the road from the church, for a swim instead of attending mass during the summer months.

One time I was skipping church, and a girl that I knew and who probably had the same idea about skipping out on something came down to go swimming. We all changed at the same place, and she showed me her developing teen breasts. This was my first good look at real boobs; neither church nor the BVM could guilt me away from that image. I finally was confirmed in the Catholic church four years later than others my age because of my truancy. It was all worth it.

The road from our farm to Lake Como was about five curvy miles once you hit the hard road below Camp Wayne—maybe four. As you broke over the hill into the village, there was a sawmill sign on the right that read, "More Cargo Is Moved on a Margo." This sign never made any sense to me. It seems that Marge was the wife of Henry Sienko, who owned the mill. If this was a compliment to his wife, I wondered what she had done to deserve it. Some folks said Hank had more money than God, but I never saw any of it and my dad said I probably never would.

If we stopped in the village, it was usually for gas. There was a small station owned by Joe Jermulsic. Joe was a good guy, a friend of Dad's from the garage days. Car mechanics speak their own language. Quickly and silently a Tootsie Roll would appear and literally jump from his large and crooked motor oil–stained hands into your pocket. He had a talent for saving face among men who knew the shame of poverty and the needs of their children. Joe's wife sat silently behind the counter, pasting green stamps in books for treasures she could only imagine.

Down the street, if you could call a paved country road a street, there was a barbershop where we got "flattop" haircuts by a guy named Mr. Williams. I think that he had one hand missing.

He would cut all us four boys' hair and Dad's, too, for two dollars. I guess his lacking one hand meant a discount for us.

Another person in the neighborhood was Charlie Clapper. People thought he was crazy. My dad said he was not crazy but suffered from a WW I gas attack and had a metal plate in his head. He could be seen talking to himself and waving his hands as he walked. I always wanted to meet him, but he died first. Anyway, he was somewhat of a hermit, and some of the kids called him the "axe man." Someone had to be it, I figure.

Sometime when I was a kid, we got a community hall built in the middle of the village right across from the Catholic church. This large building was a strange accomplishment for a rural community. If there was a specific purpose for this hall, folks did not seem to know what it was. So it became a roller-skating rink. I was not aware that farm kids had much of an interest in roller-skating, but we tried. Roller-skating may be a tutorship for future NASCAR participation for rural folks as you go around and around in a circle, bumping off of walls. The cost was low and the entertainment level high for us kids who worked most of the day and had little distractions outside of smoking and fighting our way through school. On Saturday night, the big deal was roller-skating, and a long walk home at eleven o'clock at night. It was at this time that I found some other kids who drove cars and had the magic elixir, beer and whiskey. The next few months turned into interesting years much quicker than I had anticipated.

Chapter 11

THE INTRODUCTION

ON MY FIRST BUS RIDE into New York state from Pennsylvania to begin seventh grade at Hancock Central High School, I ran into two major obstacles in addition to the bus torture: Sin City and Pat O'D. I had been to Hancock several times as a child, and basically it revolved around grocery shopping at the A&P. Folks, especially Teddy the meat man, were always friendly. Eventually Mom would get a job at the A&P and work there part-time for grocery money. I saw the streets of Sin City as paved with, at least, blacktop and this was a step up from red shale. There were stores and goods that I had never seen before. I knew that there was a world out there, and internally I had been longing for it. Even in ignorance, most kids naturally dream about having new experiences.

Seventh grade was a proving ground. I was old enough and puberty had done a fair amount of its job to prepare me for the rite of passage called junior high. I had plenty of internalized anger, but was oddly enough feeling less aggressive as the excitement and wonders of being in a new and larger environment prevailed—or so I thought. Pat O'D., God rest his soul, was a tormented man who projected his deep resentments without regard in the public school setting. Room 214 at the top of the east end of the building on the second floor was his arena. If you doubted that he was the chief gladiator, just one glance his way was considered a challenge to O'D. I was not happy that I had this "teacher" for homeroom and again for English. I secretly thought that I was crazy, but I *knew* he was. I wanted a new start where I could have a normal student and teacher relationship, but this man wanted to turn that relationship into something else. He almost succeeded.

Eventually we came to an agreement that began one morning when he decided to strut his stuff by knocking me out of my seat. Understand that O'D. needed no reason; if you were there when he began acting out, you would catch hell. Out of fear, as I went down I grabbed his necktie. Luckily for me the tie was not a clip-on, which was fashionable in those days. O'D. ended up cutting off his own breathing by pushing me down. He grabbed at my neck to stop me from falling and him from choking. We were in one of those moments when movement almost stops and feels like slow motion. Our eyes met, and somewhere in this brief encounter a nonverbal truce was made. Perhaps my many months of work on the farm paid a dividend after all. I was small but had strong hands and enough grit to not let go of the tie. I had won a standoff, and this was victory enough for me. The rest of the year stood on our agreement: I would not try to show O'D. up, and he would not bully me. This is a lesson that could have served me well had I remembered to apply it to other relationships.

The usual bullying existed in gym class, the locker room, and on the school bus, but it seemed that I quickly adjusted to avoiding clashes. My anxiety served a purpose, and I discovered when I paid attention to it I was successful in avoiding most conflicts.

I discovered that at lunch hour I could leave the school grounds and go "over town." This was a mad rush to freedom when the bell rang that I cherished, as it allowed me to see the many places that Hancock was popular for, and to smoke cigarettes.

The Central Diner was owned by J. R.'s mother and had great cheeseburgers. The mayor, who owned the Star Restaurant, was somewhat standoffish with the schoolkids but had great FF with gravy. This was also where the Short-Line and Greyhound bus stops were. Thea and John Pappas owned Kandy-Land. This place was like heaven and had everything that I craved: hamburgers and french fries with or without gravy, homemade ice cream, candy, and egg creams. John Pappas had a temper and little knowledge of English, but he would always be nice after the initial grump. I think that he worked all the time; his homemade candy was a product of his love and hard work. On Wednesdays we went to Hazen's Ice Cream Parlor and had banana splits for thirty-five cents.

My good friend Randy H. turned me on to most of the places that kids were interested in and to Hancock etiquette. Who, where, and what to avoid on certain days and times was important. In junior high we had neither money nor status, and we considered ourselves lucky to be free, so we stayed under the radar. This meant avoiding the crowds around the baseball machine in Kandy-Land that the older guys like Victor D. and David J. dominated. Not flashing our cigarettes around the older guys or staring at their girlfriends was a good idea too. There were some mistakes made as I integrated into a more or less civilized place, and there were rules and boundaries I had to learn.

Thelma's was a curios store over by Harold Baker's barbershop, and the desire of the day for most guys was a Zippo lighter. Everyone who smoked wanted one. I can't say who was guilty besides myself, but there were three of us and three lighters were stolen. As soon as I took it, I didn't want the lighter, but the desire to keep up with my friends, to be accepted by them, and to be cool around them was powerful.

By the time I had gotten home, my parents already knew about my criminal activity, and with the public phone line, so did all the neighbors. The larger lesson ended up embedded in the feeling of power that came from stealing. Attached to the act was a shot of adrenaline that overcame my timidity. I was scared shitless, yet deep inside I nurtured a Robin Hood mentality. I countered my deprivation with an immature sense of entitlement. I was a have not, and everyone else was a have.

Of course I had to go apologize to Thelma and pay the $2.50 for the lighter. I never did find where the lighter went, the booty was inconsequential. My dad had to loan me the money, which was something that he did not have much of. So much for the lesson in shoplifting. Yet I was destined to head down a one-way street that leads to trouble and life on the "edge." We smoked cigarettes on the street and would cup them in our hands when adults would drive by. All of us kids smoked, just like our parents did. Alternatives to mood altering became more popular in the '60s, so I guess in many ways I was ahead of the curve.

My obsession with Sin City and the energy I felt when in town did not erase my love for the rural life and our farm. Now, no matter what happened in Hancock, I could leave at some time and go home to the farm, the barn, and my privacy. Having options was a new experience for me, a beautiful thing. All kids need options. Saying yes is just as important as saying no; I just never knew I could.

The need for self-medication grew whenever any trauma from the past was triggered. I was in survival mode. When we were able to leave the farm on some weekend nights under the guise of attending football games at the high school, the motivation was mood alteration. At that time it was cigarettes and occasional drinks of beer or some Boones Farm wine, which was rapidly becoming infamous.

The football games bored me, and I did not know many of the kids. The truth was that I was too socially retarded to know what normal was. Throughout the next year I would bond with the proverbial tough guys who saw the local street as theirs—Victor D., Arnie S., and sometimes Billy W. and Billy L. Our thing was to hang on the corner by Frank's Market, smoke Lucky Strike cigarettes, and on weekends drink beer. Sometimes we could scrape up enough money for something stronger like blackberry brandy. Topper beer was three quarts for a dollar and Rheingold beer, whether chug-a-mugs or cans, was about $1.25 a six-pack. It is amazing what the mind can remember. My memory about times using alcohol was detailed, even then. Folks with alcoholism have memories about alcohol.

Our favorite place to drink was, oddly enough, the railroad trestle (although we could also make do in the pines by the high school or in the alley behind the movie theater). The railroad, like the river, was the reason for Hancock in the first place. The tracks ran the length of the village and crossed the river with a trestle to connect the "Brooklyn" side of Hancock to the main street area for train traffic.

These were marginalized hangouts for marginalized kids; on the edge was what we got our esteem from. These actions defined our identity or what we were not; no one else but a loser would climb down through railroad bridge railings onto an abutment over the river to drink beer. The height over the water was frightful and the view was one of shit-eddy and rocks. The conversation was mostly bullshit about the sexual activity that we never had, but could brag about in detail. We would invariably talk about the last kid who jumped or fell into the river from the small concrete pad we all shared.

When these exciting moments passed, we would head for Kandy-Land and something to eat, usually FF with gravy or if we could afford it, a hamburger too. John and Thea knew the score and would often ask us why we were not at "the game," and in their own way were looking out for us. They were great people who had more love for all the youth of Hancock than some parents did for their own. I always knew that if I was in serious trouble I could go to them and they would help.

The farm continued to deteriorate in spite of my dad's attempts to turn milk into money and my mother's continued hard work to make everything stretch further. Milk prices were at an all-time low. They both took second jobs. Dad mowed the side of the county roads, which was hard work riding a tractor and keeping the mower working in the hottest days of the summer.

This did not reduce all the other responsibilities Dad had, and he was turning haggard from doing the work of three men. I was conflicted, as I was not able to help much with some of the chores that were off limits to us kids, and I was painfully aware of the shrinking resources we had. Two incidents stood out. We got a delivery of cow feed and the deal was to either leave a check on a nail near the feed bin for the deliveryman to take with him or to send in a check within a week. Dad did neither, but claimed he did leave the check on the nail, probably to buy time. There was a conflict about this incident that ended up with us not getting a feed delivery until the check was produced. This was the first time I was confronted with my dad lying. I somehow felt responsible for this challenge to Dad's integrity. It was natural, I guess, to simply enjoin in the lie rather than stand up for what I knew was the truth. There would be consequences for this choice throughout my life.

The big kahuna was one afternoon when the head of the bank came to the house. Basically it was a replay of the old "I'm going to have to take your farm away if you don't pay the mortgage" routine. No one talked about this visit even though we all knew the consequences. It became one more unresolved elephant in the room that could not be acknowledged. The shit piled up. Believe it or not, the answer to the money problem would come from Sin City.

Chapter 12

GIRLFRIEND

MY FATHER, REALIZING THAT MILKING cows couldn't feed his family, had taken a job at the Delaware Inn bartending on weekends. I knew little about that environment—and how its impact would alter my life's direction. I would not become a dairy farmer or mechanic, or the veterinarian that I imagined I might be one day.

I walked one night to the DI after a high school dance to see my dad and to find a ride home. I was overwhelmed by what I saw. There was a large lobby with oak chairs where men and women were sitting, talking, and laughing. The barroom was full of smoke, the jukebox was wailing, and folks were playing pool and dancing. I tasted pizza for the first time. This place was fun. The scene was animated, a live movie before my eyes, yet my inner loyalty to our present way of life was challenged in ways I could not explain. There was a knot in my stomach. Was I scared? Where did this world come from; had it always been here and I had been ignorant of it? In some ways I felt betrayed.

My gut said that this was an environment to be vigilant about.

Countering my anxiety was the presence of Dad leaning against the back bar; he looked tired but content. He smiled as he waited on the thirsty customers calling to him to refill their drinks. This was not a dad that I was familiar with, and for several days the vision of him in this strange world stayed on my mind. Again, just as with the feed bill, my loyalty to my father was challenged. How could he be so different at home on the farm than he was here? The answer was money. He would bring home in tips and pay from one or two nights tending bar at the DI equal to or more than what we made on the farm in a week.

Leaving the farm was painful, but eventually we agreed that poverty was no fun, and living a life of social isolation was rapidly approaching the point of no return. On some level we were an odd bunch of personalities. Like the children of most large rural families of the sixties, we represented a varied yet distinct future culture. The world was moving with or without us, and we might as well go along for the ride. Besides, Sin City was calling.

Within a year, my dad and mom decided that we would "sell out," meaning move off the farm. We would buy the Delaware Inn from Al Schoonmaker in a partnership with the bar manager, Elton Clark. In the end, "Clarkie" decided against going in on the deal, and the Clune family bought the Delaware Inn. There now seemed to be so much I didn't know that the future seemed confusing, yet the anxiety of change was masked with excitement.

Few buildings in Hancock had the history and held the secrets of the Delaware Inn. I learned quickly that one of the significant aspects of bar and restaurant culture was gossip. Much of what was heard was embellished; dividing by eight usually landed you closer to reality. Sometimes information was germinated in one bar and eagerly carried, like birds carry seeds, by customers to the next place. Even so, this was the news of the community. What quickly came to me was that I had been socially isolated and ignorant about the workings of the world, even a world as small as this village of some fifteen hundred folks. It was with this combination of hunger for knowledge and trepidation about change that I, too, went along for the ride. It's a small world after all.

It all seemed so simple, as I observed the various routines folks used to socialize in the bar environment while I washed glasses and carried ice. The key to successful mingling seemed directly proportionate to the number of drinks a person had either bought someone or had consumed themself. Liquid courage had its limitations too, I discovered. Conversely, there also seemed to be a point of no return on the amount of investment in the other person's bar bill. The key was the alcohol, and it didn't seem to matter what the drink was—beer, wine, or cocktails. ... And of course, timing was important.

Sometimes folks played out the pick-up game for hours. Buying drinks, playing the jukebox, and engaging in a few misplayed games of pool—and someone else would come in and scoop up the prey. I watched this happen to both guys and gals. We were an equal opportunity establishment. There were the embarrassing moments too when some guy's wife or some gal's husband showed up and their significant other was flirting with someone else or being seduced themself. I watched helplessly one Friday evening when a man came in and dragged his wife out by her hair, hitting her with his other hand as he dragged her out across the lobby and through the front door. Folks shook their heads and went on drinking. I also listened as bartenders took fat tips to tell wives and husbands, on the phone, that their significant other was not there or had just left. At a later date, I too played those games as a bartender.

There were the early afternoon workers eager to part with their hard-earned money to numb the rigors of their jobs—cutting bluestone or ash bolts was often dangerous and certainly physically hard. Later on, the white-collar folks would come in. This was often a mix of guys and gals, more so on paydays, which were usually Fridays. Some left quickly to get home to significant others, others left quickly to not go home to significant others. Some were reminded by a phone call to leave the ones they loved and go home to their families. My favorites were folks who, after a couple of stiff ones, hunkered into the dreamland of their fantasies as the music of the jukebox "made the world go away." We called them chickens. They were usually willing to go with about anyone willing to take a chance. Usually by eleven or twelve they were intoxicated and a little bit guilty about responsibilities untended to. Might as well go all the way. The later it got, the better they looked!

I, too, learned that liquid lubricant gave me courage to master school social functions and found out quickly that if I slammed down a few beers, I would ask anyone to dance and dance and dance. The relationship that really impressed me, sadly, was the connection between my courage and the alcohol. The relationship and the patterns were quickly established. For the next twenty-five years, I would not have an intimate moment without liquid courage inside of me.

At sixteen I got a driver's license, a car, and a fake ID. It was a rite of passage. I validated it on a regular basis by visiting Alex Markunas, the proprietor of the Solitude Inn. The Solitude was an obscure roadhouse that was about five miles west of Hancock. Alex was always drunk, I believe over the loss of a son, yet I don't remember the details. Perhaps he welcomed us younger guys as a substitute. I don't believe that we ever thought about why it was called the Solitude. I now know that is how I felt—alone, like Alex.

By this time, my family had bought the DI, and I had one of those young adult crises: Do I work for my dad and mom or do

I work for someone else? I did both. I couldn't resist the $1.35 an hour I earned at the Victory market. It was my own money, and by then I needed it. There were times when I would sneak a drink at the bar, but I still had enough morality left to not steal from my family overtly.

Dad had bought a new 1965 Ford LTD when he found financial success in the Delaware Inn. This was the first new car I ever remember him buying, and I took pride in borrowing it. First rule was that girls liked guys with cars. I imagined that it had something to do with that parking thing that was talked about at school.

Dad only expected gas in return. It cost $7 at Knighton's to fill it up, and I even got green stamps and a glass. I wasn't sure what the glass was for, so I collected them for a while. If he ever knew what I did with that car ... A V8 engine and a sixteen-year-old boy often did not mix well; add some beer, and it was off to the races, literally. I was lucky; the only ticket I ever got with that car was trying to outrun a cop on my way to the Afton Fair one summer's evening. He said he would only ticket me for 80 mph because he couldn't tell how fast I was going on the curvy road. I went to Judge Brewer and humbly paid the $15 fine. Aside from that, I was ready—beer, a car with a big engine, and the fantasy of a gal sitting close next to me was on my mind.

By the time I was sixteen, I could no longer ignore the ongoing angst in my heart or in my pants. Girls and sex occupied my thinking, convoluted my feelings, and peppered my conversations, especially with the other guys. I often wonder if guy-speak is the same everywhere. Most of the words we used with each other were meant to be humorous and often had sexual overtones. Putting people down around their sexual orientation was common. You were either a stud or a fag; you had a handle or a wiener; you were a punk or not. Masculinity was challenged with sick remarks and hand gestures. The jokes were crude, but they took their toll on one's esteem.

I could see that the high school guys all had girlfriends; these were the role models. C&T, V&J, J&S, D&P, G&G, were just a few of the couples I saw. What I could see looked like a good deal. Hand-holding was big in public, and it seemed that this would make school more tolerable; it was someone to talk to. In cars, couples were sitting close together, and this fired my imagination. Sometimes I would see them kiss. I pondered how that tasted. Then there was "parking" which was something that I wondered about. The fogged-up windows and music which vibrated the air told me something exciting was going on in there.

In seventh grade, I had had a brief insight to the emotion we call love. Since this was something never talked about in our family, I was surprised when my mom supported me in having a girlfriend by driving me and her to the movies one Friday night. This event lasted about a week; however the fire was lit. It would burst into a blaze in the following two years.

All around me the girls who had no names and were little noticed in the past years were suddenly gorgeous! In every classroom there were blooming breasts, shorter skirts, and sweeter smiles. Some of my teachers had figures too. That did not go without notice! Could it just be me? I took elementary algebra three times, and I can now place the reason for this as the teacher's legs. Heels and stockings alone would take me to la-la-land. The girls in gym class wore tight shorts, and at pep rallies, the high school cheerleaders sported short skirts with matching underwear. They strutted around the gym, demonstrating their dexterity with splits and jumps that gave us more than a hint of leg and ass.

Perhaps the excitement was the cusp of a coming sexual revolution. I never could see how one got that excited over a football game. Looking back, I am not sure that these rituals were about scholastic moxie as much as they were about the repressed sexual spirit that was in the air. After all, the sixties were well upon us, and the realities of personal exploration of emotions and body were rapidly rolling in on us, even in Hancock.

This small community, sandwiched along the Delaware River, had three major social influences. One was an abundance of bars and restaurants that were kept profitable by nature's gifts of bluestone and hardwoods. Another was the abundance of churches that had not entered the era of community involvement; basically you went there once a week. The third was the highway that replaced the historic river and railroad traffic and brought folks into the area from more metropolitan settings like New York City, New Jersey, Philadelphia, and Connecticut. There were bars and restaurants that catered to everyone—including me and the other guys. We didn't go to the diner for just the eggs. There was obvious flirtation with the waitresses who wore tight pink uniforms and gave us attention in exchange for tips. A little bit of cleavage went a long way.

While I didn't see the school as an agent of change, it certainly was the stage where much of the new order was acted out on a daily basis. My older sister was dating guys who showed up in their flashy cars. She seemed happy as they motored away for the night in a Ford convertible or some other hot-rod. My older brother had a girlfriend from French Woods. I had neither car nor girlfriend. I learned much of my information about dating by observing others; there was no shortage of role models at HCS. I watched carefully, as imitation is the best form of flattery. The other reason I watched a lot is that I was shy. I hadn't really noticed this about myself until it came to approaching a girl to talk to her. The only pick-up line I had was "hi."

In my mind, as I watched the upper-class studs, I was sure I had it in me. I combed my hair in a jelly roll, and when that didn't work out, I got a flattop with the greased-back sides and a duck's ass do. I invested in Brylcreem. I bought tight high-water black jeans at McGranaghan's, and a pair of PR fence climbers at Marino's. I put cleats on the heels of them and walked like Victor Doolittle. Victor had a deliberate strut that made a special sound that announced him coming; he made the most music while walking the halls of HCS. He said that if you put a little Vaseline on your shoes, they would really shine. It's not easy to learn to be cool, let alone be cool. I smoked Lucky Strike cigarettes like he did; "LSMFT," I was brand loyal. I read most of the "information" written on the walls of the boys' bathroom toilet stalls and even added some prime misinformation to the mix. In spite of a valiant effort, I couldn't put it all together. I was lost. There were opportunities that came my way to be appropriately social and have a girlfriend, and I got almost lucky a few times, but not while I was sober.

My first real experience with my misunderstood feelings of love happened by chance, but the memory remains with me somewhat to this day. If you look at the demographics of the Hancock area, there are lots of Italians, Irish, and a mixture of Germans, Swedes, Dutch, and mutts like myself. The area was white, European, with a mix of Yankees and a bit of Native American. This girl was Italian, and I was stung. Not the dark-skinned, black hair Italian, but one with lighter brown hair and a Roman profile. I would call her "striking" today, as I remember her that way.

I was at the Delaware Inn one summer day, sitting on the porch, when two girls strolled by. The sidewalk, which was on the same level as the porch, allowed a perfect view for girl watching. One girl was a leggy blonde, Barbie-ish, which was cool for the day (she ended up marrying a good friend of mine). The other was a cute brunette with short hair, something that always attracted me. I remember it was hot that day and she was wearing shorts, tan in color, and a T-shirt with the short sleeves rolled up. She had shapely legs, perky breasts, and she was short, like me. Her smile said she liked me. There was the look—back and forth—the shining eyes, the kind of electricity that goes right to the heart of the matter. Whether you are fifteen or sixty, the rising passion is the same.

I did the usual underground friend-of-a-friend gossipy investigation at school and got her name. "F" lived in Hancock and was the only child of a local businessman and a very protective mother. I mention this because normally when two kids connect they can meet at school, maybe have lunch together, and sometimes would be able to meet after school or at a dance or some other activity. Or so I thought. This wasn't going to happen, as this only child was hawked by her mother, with assistance from an aunt, from the day they caught on to us. So the relationship never really matured even though we kept in touch for many years. A few notes were passed, a kiss here and there, but I was four years older than her and off to college by the time she had the freedom to "date." Anyway, it was never to be.

After I graduated from college, I was working in Binghamton, New York, as a cook; this was the closest city to Hancock. She attended the local community college. One day I drove her to a store in downtown Binghamton (where she first met her future husband). I was still nurturing fantasies—"white-picket lust" was the usual narrative that played out in my "Ozzie and Harriet" mind-set—where we would get married and have a nice house with two kids, two cars, spontaneous sex (at the kitchen sink or on the table), and have a nightly ritual doing the dishes together. And all this would be surrounded with a white picket fence. Fat chance. I saw her give this guy who was parking cars the same look that she had given me years earlier, and I knew then and there that it was over. I was out of the running. Life is a deck of jokers.

The point is that the feelings were intense, the desire was overwhelming, and the fantasy was … well … fantastic. This narrative followed me around for many years and continued to repeat itself in many relationships; I could probably conjure it up right now in the right circumstances. Early learning is a very powerful reinforcement for later life. When we are in real love, we want the person's goodness. When in lust, you only want the person's body—sometimes briefly, sometimes regularly. In codependent love, the emotions get so confusing you can't love either. I was stuck on third.

Chapter 13

AT THE END OF THE ROAD

HANCOCK IS BOTH A VILLAGE and a larger town; on the west and south it hugs the neighboring county lines and the river, which borders Pennsylvania. The larger area includes the smaller hamlets and crossroads like Hale Eddy, Cadosia, East Branch, Fish's Eddy, Peas Eddy, and Sands Creek, and it stretches across the Delaware River into Pennsylvania to include Winterdale. I was a roamer by nature, and this was my "territory." I was happiest when going somewhere to do something, and always eager to see new things and, of course, meet new people. My driver's license was a much-awaited rite of passage, if only to serve those needs. I always liked cars and in some ways have been obsessed by them—but not like some of the local young mechanics like Jack Daily were, since I couldn't turn a wrench. I liked different designs, and eventually cars that were from Europe caught my attention; my fondness was for English and German engineered machines. At that time in my life I sought freedom, not unlike most every other youth.

To the west, Hale Eddy was one of the small hamlets that became isolated by the Rockefeller expansion of highways in New

York state in the 1960s that included Route 17. There were several small cottages along the river at the Eddy, a couple of motels on the westbound side of the highway, and a bridge that allowed you to cross the Delaware River there.

The only family I knew that lived there was the Davidson family. Mr. Davidson, or R. J. as he was known among students, was the guru of advanced math classes at Hancock Central High School. I had him for homeroom in tenth grade, which included an attendance ritual and a study hall at the end of the day. His expectations for performance in math class excluded me, as understanding math was one of the learning disabilities I did not know I had. R. J. had a crust about himself, yet as one of our class advisors, he allowed some of us to dig inside and appreciate his sense of humor and his view of the world. I have the pleasure of knowing his daughters Lizzie and Maggie, and I see him in their personalities.

I sometimes launched my canoe at the Hale Eddy bridge for some fishing as I floated to Hancock or farther downriver if the season was right. The west branch of the Delaware River was a meandering constant, patiently following the highway. It was one of the few unchanging beauties that made Hancock attractive. Route17 was a two-lane road that began at the New York/New Jersey border on its east end and ran west to Jamestown and Chautauqua, ending at Lake Erie.

Once Route17 became a major road, much of the economic means bypassed rural towns like Hancock, and folks stopped for their needs in larger cities. The time to get anywhere was now shortened by added lanes and faster speed limits. A four-lane highway was a big deal then. This literally took the food from the mouths of folks who made a living from the traffic that went through towns like Hancock. When you crossed into Pennsylvania from Hancock, New York, on the main bridge at Route191, you would be in what is commonly known as Hancock, Pennsylvania. Stay left and you go through Stockport and eventually into Equinunk. Bear to the right and you are in a small settlement of homes that are in Pennsylvania, yet share the common village across the river in New York. I imagine that folks settled there in the sixties because of the expensive tax rates in Hancock. Someone had to pay for that highway. My friends Randy and Robin live there. So did the "Z" man (John Zawatsky), another teacher and coach, who was always kind and understanding. Continue on and you are in Winterdale, Pennsylvania, one of the poorest places in the area. There are trailers drawn together with a common roof and lots of junk cars. It appears as if Larry the Cable Guy could be comfortable there. There was immense poverty in this backcountry valley, yet the folks I knew there were resourceful and hard working. They did business with a handshake (although some of them had crossed fingers at times).

The nearest hamlet to Hancock on the east side is Cadosia, then Fish's Eddy, and finally East Branch, as you continue east on Route 17. These are hamlets that existed on the trade of hardwood timber, the railroad, and bluestone that young and old prospected for in the surrounding hills. When you look east upriver from the dug road near Cadosia in the late afternoon, with the sun over your back, the water glistens off the rocks and throws up hues of yellow and green. Sometimes there are miniature rainbows that tease. In the winter months, the view is framed by snow on the surrounding hills and patches of frozen water near the shoreline where the liquid runs quieter. This picture remains in my mind as one of the most beautiful images of nature at work on the east branch of the Delaware River.

Cadosia, I believe, was originally a settlement of railroad workers. There was a large depot and a mill that made railroad ties, and these drew a large immigrant population that came to build and maintain the Erie-Lackawanna Railroad. When I was a teenager, it was also a community with a majority of Italians, many from the old world. One time after school on a Friday, Peter Salvadore invited me to his home above Marino's store. The smell of a stew I never have forgotten that he called "peas and eggs" was in a large pot on the stove. I have never been able to imitate such delicious and authentic Italian cooking. Another time I went with Greg Possemato to his grandmother's house in Cadosia at Thanksgiving time. Mama mia!! I tasted food that was deep and rich; homemade noodles and sausages, and a sauce that they referred to as "gravy." Italian history on a plate in real time. These women were full of ethnic pride in an affirming way that drew you in with their cooking and generosity.

At Fish's Eddy, an exit off Route 17, there was Freddie's Diner, a classic country eatery. It was pretty much a place where loggers and stonecutters stopped on their way to the various sawmills in the area or to one of the stone docks in East Branch. Characters that will always be part of the spoken history owned many of these local businesses; they were rich with personality.

If you cross the Delaware out of Hancock on Route 97, you are headed south along the main river, and if you take an immediate left at the bowling alley, you are on the Peas Eddy Road. This small slice into the hills of Hancock was a natural beauty that remained unmolested as the river hugged the embankment of a gravel-surface road on one side. Across the road was the steepness of the mountains. The woods there sheltered many unspoiled nooks and crannies of wood and wildlife. I often walked the hills overlooking the river on the southeastern slope, and I could see all the way east to Hawk's Mountain from above Eel Wire Hollow.

I would lie in the sun on warm ground that was provided by an opening between the many leafy trees. On my back, watching the clouds float by pleased me. On that mountain, life made sense. The sky was up and I was there, grounded; the smell of my surroundings was in the very air I breathed. Sometimes I would fall asleep, to be aroused by the cooling of the sun retreating westward. Waking up, I had the clarity of purpose and a sense of self not found in any crowd of human noise and garble.

At sixteen, my spiritual persona was at war with my biology and social self. I needed mentoring, and if there is a higher power, he spoke to me there. Many times I have gone up those paths to be alone and watch the hawks and eagles glide on the unseen wind current that sweeps along the river in the valley. I envied them mostly. Maturation is its own timepiece. When you are in the process, you cannot slow down enough to observe what is really going on, let alone control it. I was a teenage dervish, whirling to an unseen and often unheard sound. I was spinning free. My dreams today are filled with pleasure of those moments. There is much pleasure in the recall, as bringing memories to the present moment makes them real over and over. Although I am not physically there in time or space, my feelings and emotions can be. Today I value that.

On the other side of the coin, much of the time during those years was spent self-medicating. In spite of all the wonderful thoughts and beautiful dreams, I always ended up in the same place—drunk on some cheap-ass swill at eighty-seven cents a fifth, smoking some "home grown" alleged-to-be Panama Red, and/or tripping my ass off, or worse. I also liked pills, as they seemed somewhat legitimate. Cigarettes added to the numbness. My depression and anxiety revealed little about abuse of past years. The trauma was like a threesome of crows watching, waiting, and pecking away at me piece by piece like some carcass along the road. I could chase them away briefly, but they quickly returned.

My saving grace at that time was work. Any kind of work was fine if you let me work independently. I couldn't drive a nail straight with someone watching me. Authority issues, I assume. Work gave me the access to money, which gave me an attribute to hide behind. I needed to interact socially, and drugs and booze protected me from the reality of how cruel folks were and the hatred they carried for their fellow persons. From behind the mask, I could safely observe; it was how I learned, I watched.

During that summer of '66 I ran into a "blondie" from New Jersey as I was cruising Hancock's west Main Street. I beeped the horn and she waved. The first time we actually spoke was in Kandy-Land. She approached me. It is difficult to describe, and I wish that I could manufacture the intense combination of anxiety and excitement at these moments; while they are primitive, they can be sophisticated at the same time. These universal thoughts and feelings continue to thrive in the most squalid and inhospitable places. There is no name for them. Synergistically they combine into the dyad humans call love. How simplistic.

Someone else from somewhere new always intrigued me, and it didn't hurt that this girl was a teenager. While I found her accent different, she was cute and somewhat shy like myself, I discovered. Her family had a large old house on the green flats road that was, for me, the way a summerhouse should look—grayed, old single-pane windows needing paint, large rooms, wooden floors, and casually comfortable furnishings. The river was about twenty yards away, and a cool breeze blew away the crustiness of hot, humid summer days. There was beer in a large tin bucket full of ice and a campfire on the lawn, and cars and trucks were parked at random. The family was friendly and welcoming yet did not pry or seem to be annoyed by my presence. I felt comfortable because they were comfortable, a benefit of vigilance if you pay attention to your inner survivor self. Although her mom had one eye on us, we were able to spend a good amount of time walking in the woods, holding hands, putting our feet in the river, throwing rocks, and making out. Her name was Liz, which suited me fine, and I visited her often that summer. This was a distraction that I needed.

At that time, Hancock had a real movie theater called the Capitol. Buzzy, the owner, kept it in good condition, and we went to the movies there whenever we could. This was a good place to sit in the balcony and make out away from others. My behavior, mostly guided by hormones, cars with large motors, and the need for attention, quickly overwhelmed any oppositional mores or Catholic lectures in the face of potential hoo-haw. Fortunately or not, there had been little modeling or information given to us about relationships in my family; mainly I proceeded on emotions. I realize now that this was not some psychotic scheme, but I was behaving in a normal teen fashion. I did lack guidance however. Fifteen-year-old girls' behavior also seemed to be guided by hormones, guys with cars with large motors, and a need for attention.

The dynamic for bringing us guys and gals together differed philosophically, both then and now to a lesser extent. We "guys" were always supposed to be "ready" to pursue; as most gals lived with the pallor of "the reputation myth." This dissonance kept us apart at first. I expected this to be played out as rejecting the guy's advances, at least in public. The way to get attention was to pretend that you did not want it. What's that about? Guys characterize this as "playing hard to get." Girls call this being "coy."

While the girl-and-boy friendship lasted most of the summer,

I visited her in New Jersey a couple of times over the winter, and we remained friends. One of the positive aspects of our relationship was that we talked about our feelings; each had opinions that were different, yet respected. Communication was new ground for me, a functional process! Several years later, she showed up at my apartment when I was living in Syracuse, New York. She was fleeing from a domestic abuse situation, and I was happy to help her out. I hope today that she is safe and content.

Here is another war story. My friend E. and I discovered that the green flats road extended beyond Liz's family's house and dead-ended at Peas Island. On the left were a couple of houses, one large and at least one smaller cottage type. Somehow we discovered that two teen "chicks" from Rochester, New York, stayed in the small cabin for the summer and the adults occupied the larger house. At times, the girls were there alone. So E. and I agreed to meet them—bolstered with some liquid courage—to "party." E. seemed much more advanced than I was at social interaction that is often mislabeled as intimacy. I felt like I had achieved some success, although getting laid for the first time is … well, overrated; at least it was for me. Unfortunately the cabin bunks were somewhat old and dirty, and within two days I had a case of the "crabs." If you do not like bugs and are inclined to be somewhat obsessive, especially around hygiene, this can really creep you out. It did me. I went to see my confidential pharmacist and plastered myself with what was some form of alcohol-based smelly liquid that would qualify as bio-fuel.

To heap misery on top of misery, I was walking by the Capital Lounge the next day and saw my friend E. in his uncle's car. Now mind you, remember what I said about white picket lust; and in spite of taking home some pets unannounced, I was enthralled by this babe. Tina, whose last name slips my tongue gladly and remains in my memory ungladly, duped me. I waved to E. and saw a blonde head in the passenger seat bobbing for apples. As I moved closer to say, "What's up," I realize he is with Tina, the girl I had been with the day before. These behaviors have no meaning to teenage guys, so we label them as buddy fucking. Once again I am disappointed and extremely self-critical. I can again justify getting blasted. My esteem and self-pity were doing battle. Self-pity was winning. I had not yet discovered that while certain folks are optimal company, self-esteem is exactly as it sounds—an inside job. This was the first time that the big S crossed my mind. I was smiling at them from outside the car, acting cool and at the same time thinking, *I am a piece of shit.* The contradiction would be so apparent to anyone else except me. I knew I had a problem regulating my feelings, but I just did not see what that problem was yet.

There had been moments in my junior year of high school, when I am sure a problem was apparent. When I was the master of ceremonies for our junior prom, I was drunk. The evening was meaningless. I had a date who was doing me a favor. I was there, numb and dumb, all dressed up with nowhere to go. The farce continued. The fact is, I could pull it off. Being surrounded with many like-minded and similarly behaving individuals was a bonus; there was camouflage in large numbers, and someone always looked worse off than me. Thousands of wildebeests cross the Zambezi River together each dry season. Crocodiles eat a few when they stray from the pack. Most go unnoticed. Stay in the middle of the pack Dan, and you'll survive.

There was rising rage from rejection and betrayal that I pushed down with whatever booze was available. Beer would do, a lot of it would do it better. I would drive from East Branch where I could drink at the old Beaver-Dell Hotel, to Davidson's bar on the other side of Deposit. I really did not know what nomadic drive propelled me. Rather than discover the source of my angst,

I sought out other unfamiliar places with new people. Here in my fantasy I could start over; maybe this time I could avoid being abandoned. These visits included trips to such exclusive establishments as the Dewdrop Inn and the Bucket of Blood and the Solitude Inn. Truly they were accurately named. Later on, I began prowling the low bottom bars of Clinton Street in Binghamton, where a beer and a shot was fifty cents. I thought I was someone grand, buying drinks for those guys, most of whom would piss down their legs rather than miss a round by leaving their bar stool to use the men's room.

In my senior year of high school, I excelled in English and not much else. Most teachers showed little concern. R. J., Mrs. Hall, and Mrs. Lester were exceptions. I knew that they knew that I knew that they knew; this negative contract was never spoken about aloud. I once went to the Halls' house with their son Gus. His parents were gone, so we upped a fifth of Clan McGregor—a fancy name for cheap scotch. I do remember falling down the steps to their family room and ralphing. Taste aversion is a powerful reinforcement. I never drank scotch again.

I scored the lead in the senior play, the highlight of my high school years. There was some competition for the role, but the play was "The Many Loves of Dobie Gillis," authored by Max Schulman. Who else would be more appropriate? This year went well for me, and I only got beaten up occasionally. One time it was a sucker punch to the side of my head in gym class. I went down; my chin was glass and I did not like fighting. I was on the cross-country team and the track team, and I usually ran at the middle of the pack. I never was the star, but that was fine. I just enjoyed the feel of the ground and the movement of my body as I ran. I began to feel less depressed after running. While I ran, I was able to think in complete sentences; I worked through questions that otherwise were clouded with mixed emotions. Today I know that

I was fighting my depression with physical activity. Why hadn't anyone thought of endorphins before?

On our traditional senior trip to Washington, DC we drank on the bus to Washington, drank in the hotel rooms while there, and slept on the trip back. The most exciting moment was talking John F. off the window ledge of his hotel room while he was drunk. We couldn't find any girls. Some fun, huh kids? Graduation was a blur. Any scholarships available were sucked up by students who actually cracked a book. I was left alone, undecided about what to do with my life.

After being turned down for the Army and the Navy, I passed on the Marines. Only my friends Randy Hazen and Bruce Piesecki were crazy enough for that trip, and they were promptly shipped off to Vietnam; later, Bruce re-upped. About this time there was change in the air. Teens were letting their hair grow, wearing bell-bottom jeans, arguing politics with their families, and questioning the older guard. Hancock began to respond to the new generation. Soon we would have a "head shop" and stylish sixties clothing store in Hancock thanks to the courage of Dixie and Danny Coe. The discussion about substances would move from alcohol to drugs and, of course, marijuana. The year was1969, which ended up being very symbolic; there was something happening about thirty-five miles downriver from Hancock.

White Lake, New York, is where I ended up for five days, smashed as a gourd, tripping out with lots of hippies. It may be trite to say this, however, things changed forever after that. Sex, drugs, and rock and roll were now legitimate. Woodstock was a brand name. I could ignore the guilt for the drugs and alcohol I was abusing. Parallel, however, to that behavior was the feeling that I was racing down a slippery road to addiction. Why pay attention to it now? I didn't

I took one shot for my pain, one drag for my sorrow; I'll get messed up today, I'll be ok tomorrow. (Bruno Mars—"Liquor Store Blues")

Chapter 14

WHEN THE MUSIC STOPPED

It was about the second weekend in August 1969, a week that was filled with excitement and anticipation because a "rock concert" was coming to the area. This was an unusual event for many of us who were just beginning to understand the meaning of music as the announcement of a social revolution. Before Woodstock, there was music, yet after Woodstock, there was another evolution in music taking place. The rage of the sixties was unleashed. Social justice, peace, and equality had found a voice.

I had an 8-track tape player in my car and vinyl in a large wooden box in my room at the Delaware Inn that said Bell Dairy on the side. Rocky Bell delivered milk to the hotel, and I commented on the box; the next day I found it by my car. He was that type of guy. I really liked the combination of rock and big band sounds, as well as the softer music of the folk and folk rock of the day. The confrontational songs of Dylan and Richie Havens moved me. Any music that heralded the revolution against social norms got my attention.

When I had driven to White Lake the week before on rumor of

Woodstock being moved to that location, my concept of size and depth was severely warped. Looking over a huge field, there was a beehive of folks building a stage and other towerlike constructions, with cranes and other equipment. One would not imagine what was going to happen there within a few days' time. My plan was to pitch a tent near some wooded area and set up a campsite. I must have been thinking that a few hundred people would be there. It ended up being a few hundred thousand!

By Thursday night, all hell had broken loose. My memory is thin about specifics. I remember walking up a gravel road adjacent to the field. Police were polite and no one asked me for tickets or checked my pack. There were little booths setting up along the road, and folks were selling souvenirs, tie-dyed T-shirts and posters that spoke of peace and love. People were everywhere and were being directed one way into this large field that had been empty a week ago. I was quite shocked to hear guys and gals selling marijuana, poke-a-dot and blotter acid, various other "types" of LSD, mescaline, and hash. Some cats were selling beer and wine out of coolers. Capitalism has deep roots.

I had never been exposed to such large crowds before. I certainly was naive about the extent of drug use and had two bottles of Boone's Farm apple wine in my pack to drink. Some folks—about a hundred—were right where I planned to camp, so I squeezed in my pack and a sleeping bag and introduced myself. They were all smoking pot. I had not done well with pot the few times I tried it; the anxiety I felt from smoking it was not worth the high for me.

I had heard of many of the bands by name and had some of the records they recorded. On Friday, after sleeping on the ground in the middle of the thousands of folks who continued to pour in, I enjoyed Richie Havens, a favorite of mine, and Arlo Guthrie. I was not impressed with the rest of the lineup that day, and several key folks that I wanted to see had either canceled or been booked elsewhere since they thought that this concert would be a bust.

That night it rained. While Saturday morning was wet, Saturday afternoon hosted some sunshine and turned out to be a phenomenal parade of folks, some of whom were famous and some who were not as popular yet. Santana blew everyone away. His music was fresh. Janis Joplin had everyone up and grooving to her special voice; her music made the hair on my neck stand up. I lay around that afternoon, listening to Canned Heat and the Who. While the Who played on, I must have fallen into a deep sleep.

During this long and needed rest, I dreamed a strange but somewhat familiar dream. Buzzy Goff and I had run away from Hancock. Buzzy was this taller, thin, somewhat introspective guy who even I could get along with. Easy going on the outside, it was not apparent what was driving him on the inside. We were in eleventh grade and had little interest in school besides Doris Chamberlain's class. It was one of those times when not much was happening for either one of us. One of those days, Buzzy had a case of the ass. We were goofing around and decided, let's go somewhere else; we decided that *Canada* was the answer to our angst! The motivation for this trip arose from boredom and was decided over a couple of beers—Molson Canadian of course. The bottom line is that we were stirring for some action, and Buzzy wanted to send his family the same message that I did: If we were gone, would you even know it?

I would like to say it was my original idea, but I think I remember him saying; "Let's take off to Canada!" And my reply was, "When do you want to leave?" It turned out to be the next day. Buzzy had a 1950s Oldsmobile. I cannot recall the model, but the trunk was large enough to swim in. A couple with one small child could probably have lived in the cavernous backseat alone. We loaded up one case of beer, my .410 shotgun, some shotgun shells, and about six packs of cigarettes. Buzzy had some mean-looking deer rifle (probably a .303 British) and some ammo. We both had fishing gear and most of our worldly possessions with room to spare in the trunk. After all, we were going north to the great wilderness. Thinking the fantasy through was not our forte.

We grabbed a map at Knighton Peter's Sunoco, gassed up the Olds, and pointed north. I believe that we threw a dart into the map, and it landed near enough to a village named Almonte. Of course, this was on the other side of the world to us, two rural sixteen-year-olds. Being young and adventurous (and dumb), we never thought about the guns or ammo in the trunk. Just the reality of what we had in the trunk should have triggered some anxiety, but it didn't. We felt justified.

Buzzy told the customs officers at the Thousand Islands border crossing that we were visiting his aunt in Almonte. We got one funny look as an officer screwed up his moustache, possibly in response to our mispronunciation of where we were going. Lord knows why, but he waved us through without looking in the trunk, and off the big V-8 cruised.

If you ever run away from home, the first piece of advice is please leave a note. I dreamed we did; yet while dreams are some of the most vivid recollections, they are often out of sync. We did not tell anyone except Ray Jenson; on some level we felt safe with this. I think Ray told the whole high school.

Almonte turned out to be a mill town of about twenty-five thousand on a small river north of Ottawa. Looking back, I can see it was a pretty straight line north. A town this size was twenty-five times larger than Hancock, so we did not explore much that first day as night was upon us and we were not sure of exactly where we were. We found a small cabin-type motel, and of course this and everything else was different there. The cabins felt rustic, yet this appealed to us because we felt like we were pioneers. We spent that first night talking about what our parents would do. By the time we were on our second or third beer, we were quite cocky in our remarks, vowing to never return to Hancock. I believe that the rent was $28 for the week, the dollar at that time being worth about $1.50 Canadian. At that point we were staying forever. North of the border it gets colder earlier, which means that when we left Hancock it was fall, and in Almonte it was early winter. The gas space heater in the cabin couldn't keep up with the temperature drop. Our sense of accomplishment and false bravado kept us warm, but not for long.

Actually there was no reason for me to run away from home. If there was, I couldn't really put my finger on it. Our family had been living at the Delaware Inn about a year, and maybe I was pissed off about leaving the farm. I didn't need much of an excuse in those days, just flexing probably. At the inn, I had my own room, so I cannot use the excuse of feeling crowded. Up in Almonte, a couple of days went by and soon my Irish guilt battled leaving with my Polish stubbornness, or vice versa. That second voice said "stay."

Truth travels with time, and all the justifications we had for the adventure in the first place didn't hold up for long. When the water in the cabin froze on the fourth morning, our attitudes changed; our comparisons with and rationalizations about a negative home environment grew weaker. Besides, we were out of beer, and while hot dogs have their place (which is "on occasion"), I was tired of being unsettled. So we made the phone call. In my dreams, our parents had this big powwow and wanted us back. However my dad was not impressed. He was "not mad" and was "glad I called," and we would "talk about it" when I got home. This conversation sealed the deal. "Let's go home!" we said in unison.

I think that Buzzy probably caught more crap than I did,

because his family was stricter. The best part was that even our schoolmates missed us, and the principle was nice about the whole thing. We all had a good laugh about our week off. Many of our other friends were living vicariously through our trip, and we made their week meaningful too. That felt like a bonus!

When I woke up from the dream, it was raining on and off. Night came quickly, and by morning the field was a sea of mud. I had intentions of going to sleep in my car but never made it. The folks from Rochester, New York, had a tarp strung up and a half dozen botas of wine they were sharing. They said I was talking in my sleep, so I told them the story just like it really happened three years before! Funny how memory recall works when you screw with the synapses.

Although Sunday had the hardest rain, the music was hotter than ever. Jefferson Airplane was dynamite; Joe Cocker, who did not sing out of tune, followed them. Blood, Sweat, and Tears, followed by Ten Years After, followed him. I remember Sunday as a mellow day. Someone had brought some sandwiches from a store up the road where everyone went to take a shower or to use the john, as the "portos" were mostly full. We all ate in silence like we had just experienced something unique and blissful. We knew it had to come to an end. Several attempts were made to replicate this coming together, yet to this day, not so.

Chapter 15

TALES FROM THE INN

THE DELAWARE INN WAS KNOWN for miles around for its hospitality, food, and drink. When I arrived there in tenth grade, there were some very strange folks living in and hanging around the hotel. I had trouble getting my mind and my feelings around this huge space that was home to so many others and would be my home for the next twenty years.

I lived in room twelve, which was on the third floor. For some reason, maybe because it had its own shower, I had joined those folks who live outside of the traditional bounds of family. Living in an isolated hotel room, going downstairs to a dining room to eat, and finding my socks and clothing mixed with a large number of sheets and bedspreads in the communal clothes dryer. My room had twelve-foot ceilings and a transom over the door to let heat in or out, depending on the time of the year and the condition of the steam boiler deep in the basement. I painted it purple.

On the ground floor was a lobby with some nice mission oak

chairs that creaked and groaned when sat upon, even though they had been buttressed by replacement wood screws and some wire. All in all, they were sturdy and unique. The backs were slatted and the seats had a kind of "almost leather" that was mustard in color. The area where your ass went was already well demarcated; you couldn't miss when sitting down. There were some that were rockers too. Both types of chairs would be out on the front porch in the summer and later in the afternoon had to be brought indoors. These chairs were probably fifty to seventy-five years old.

The floor was a black-and-white checkerboard pattern of rubber tile that was somewhat old fashioned, but in character with the rest of the building. The tiles had been walked on and mopped probably thousands of times, and I often wondered as I rocked in one of the chairs what those tiles had observed over the years. In the corner of the lobby was a Hancock telephone booth that could be answered on an extension behind the bar.

The front desk was a counter about four feet high with a top that was dark brown and had its share of former hotel guests' names carved in it. It fronted one of the older fireplaces that had been out of use for many years. There were ornate covers over the hearths, and the dust bunnies and occasional spider had found a home there in the crevices. The key boxes sat on the mantle, and there were the usual old-fashioned hotel-type keys with large plastic tags that had the number of the room on them. In some ways, this gave the inn its legitimacy as a hotel. Its history revealed that the Hotel Shanley, the hotel's former name a hundred years ago, was a place where the train brought people to sell and shop. It was probably one of the original "malls" as shopkeepers set up their wares to sell to folks traveling into the town to find store-bought goods.

A pressed-tin ceiling with a classic design graced the lobby. If you looked carefully, there were places where the steam pipes went through the metal and left shadows of condensation and rust-colored water had dyed the tin. The most attractive part of the lobby was the staircase. It was five feet wide and made of dark mahogany with oak treads; the dark stain complemented the rest of the room. Two large ceiling fans gave it the pseudo-Casablanca appeal, if your imagination was intact or you had enough alcohol in you.

One of the first things that caught my eye while I stood behind the front desk was the view of the railroad tracks and the depot across west Front Street through six-foot-high windows. Opposite the depot on the north side of the tracks was a three-sided shack that had a bench in it. Perhaps it was where folks traveling west sat as they waited for the passenger train. By the time we moved to Hancock, the passenger train was no longer running, yet freight trains ran several times a day. If you sat in the lobby, you did not have to see the train; you could actually feel it coming. It was like the beginning of an earthquake that rumbled closer at a steady pace then passed and disappeared, often speeding more than fifty miles per hour.

As I watched out the large front windows, I would see what appeared to be a hunched-over man dart out from behind the waiting shed and pull his head back in as if he was part of a mechanical apparatus or like a stork that thrusts and pulls its neck back quickly. I got so I could almost predict his movements before he came into my line of sight or like he knew I was watching him, which of course I was. He wore a hat that angled down in front, and he had a habit of pulling off the dirty brown brogan and rubbing his head, slapping it back on, and pulling his head back behind his little hideout. Sometimes he would take a few steps into view and say something to himself or to an imagined friend. When he ventured out further, you could see something sticking out of his coat pocket. The coat was brown, or just dirty like his hat. His hand pulled out what looked like a bottle, flat with a metal screw cap that reflected the sunlight; like a pint bottle of liquor. All day he could be seen pacing back and forth like he was expecting a train that was late.

I found out that his name was Jack. Jack the Ripper was the name folks called him, and he had worked on the railroad for many years, perhaps in the station (the information was unclear). He could not bring himself to leave the grounds except for brief jaunts to the local liquor store. Jack would purchase what probably was a liquid diet. Sometimes he slept in the waiting shack; however, any attempts to engage him ended up with Jack moving quickly away and muttering incoherently. I did not know it at the time, but he was the first floridly psychotic man I had ever met; his medication was in the bottle in his pocket. Amazing how resourceful folks can be.

The Delaware Inn, commonly known as the DI, had employees who came with the building. The janitor's duties were done by Earl Swartwout Sr. who lived in room number seven at the top of the stairs. He was an older man who had his grandson Junnie living with him. Earl took care of Junnie as well as any parent could. I think that Junnie and I were about the same age, and we got along well. Each morning Earl would sweep and mop and wipe everything clean. Then he would sweep off the front porch and the sidewalk, or when needed, hose it down. Earl rarely smiled, and he rarely minced words. I am not sure that our buying the inn from the former owner was an easy change for him. We learned to respect each other, and he seemed to like my dad. Earl would always want to "match quarters" with you. I believe he had a two-headed quarter, because it seemed like he never lost. When Earl could no longer work, we missed him. His spirit stayed at the inn long after he passed. Junnie went on to marry and have a family; they live in Cadosia.

There were the boarders who came with the hotel. Most worked construction on the highway, and some had local sawmill jobs. One of the more colorful guys was Little Lee. Little Lee got his name from his affiliation with a man called Lee, who was the boss on a construction job, building Route 17 past Hancock. It seemed Little Lee sucked up to big Lee to guarantee work for himself as a laborer. The guys on the construction job tagged him with the name and it stuck. Little Lee was ticklish, and he was often grabbed and tickled by the other men in the barroom as a joke. Little Lee was an imp and would play any gambling game available; he was always ready to play pool for money or play "liar's poker" with dollar bills. He often pulled pranks on the other construction workers who lived in the hotel. His voice was like a cackle, and most folks did not mind having him around, somewhat like a mascot. Eventually his luck ran out, and he was stabbed to death in a barroom near Clearwater, Florida, according to rumor.

Another character who lived at the DI was a guy named Kenny. Kenny's claim to fame was sleeping with a cigarette in his mouth and burning holes in the bedspread. He had a hygiene issue too. He always walked and talked like a "stud fifty-fiver" from another time and place, with a cigarette hanging out of his mouth as he spoke. Tony Gisoldi lived at the inn also. Tony had lost one foot in an accident while working on Cannonsville Dam. He was always a gentleman and eventually married a local schoolteacher, his second marriage. His father, Alex, was the shoe cobbler in Hancock and had a store on Main Street. After Tony married, he moved into his wife's house in Hancock. He would stop by from time to time just to say hi.

During those days, I basically went to school and worked at the Victory Market after classes and in the kitchen at the Delaware Inn washing dishes and learning to cook from the various folks and from my mother, who herself was a fantastic cook. Our head cook was a large woman of Mexican descent named Isabel, who would call my dad Mr. Cluney. She could do justice to most items on the menu, except soups and sauces. These items mostly fell to my mother to make; Lottie could make stone soup that tasted good.

The kitchen was ramshackle and worn down, the back porch sagged and needed replacement. Empty beer bottles were stored there in cases for pick-up. The back room was an office that kept the liquor secure, and we had a large safe of unknown origin that came from the railroad. The floor was uneven, and old calendars from past years were tacked to the walls. Underneath sheaves of paper, there was a nice antique hard maple desk.

Running the bar was Elton Clark, a veteran bartender and jack of many trades. He was an accomplished photographer and in spite of having one lung removed as a young man, Elton still lives in Hancock and is older than ninety. The last I heard, he was still driving. Elton was a pool shark and probably the best pool player in the state. He shunned playing with amateurs and could not stand to lose, which he rarely did. His responsibilities in addition to tending bar during the daytime, included ordering the beer and liquor from the various salesmen. At night Charlie Rock came to tend bar at 6 p.m. On busy weekend evenings, we had several people who helped part-time, as the bar was very busy during those days. Charlie Rock was a real gentleman. Both he and "Clarkie" taught me much about bartending and the bar/ restaurant business.

We had a chambermaid named Liz Green, who did the rooms. She and my mom took care of the laundry and the cleaning of rooms. Linen was changed regularly, and the boarders paid between $15 and $25 per week, depending on the type of room they had. Some rooms had bathrooms and some had shared baths in the hall.

This was my new home, yet the idea of living in a hotel was difficult. On one hand, it was a step up on the food ladder; going back to the farm was not an option. On the other side, what connection to, or of, family that I had was now separated into separate rooms with locks and keys. We ate singly, alone or with some of the help. There were many new foods that I was not familiar with, and there was plenty to eat. I missed the farm and would rather have had less and still be together as a family. We didn't grieve. "Buck up and get used to it," my parents would say. Their excitement about the promise of a new life was something I did not want to deflate, and I didn't want them worrying about me. They certainly didn't have time to. Over the next several years I would come and go.

Chapter 16

HIGHER LEARNING—1967

THE YEAR I GRADUATED FROM Hancock Central I was faced with a serious dilemma. I had a degree in mechanical drawing and little else. My overall grade was a gifted C from Mr. Carnahan, who just shook his head at my work. The problem I had was conceptualizing a three-dimensional drawing. My skill level was that of a stick-drawing adolescent; that's how my brain worked. The anxiety of feeling stupid and unequal, some remnants from the farm experience, some brain damage from the explosion at the Lakewood Garage, and the trauma of the hospital stay and surgeries all affected my self-esteem and my confidence.

I wanted to be a leader and was not even a good follower. I fantasized a lot, often creating success scenarios in my head to counter my feelings of inadequacy. The knowledge of learning disabilities was nil at that time, so no one could even guess what my shortcomings were. I worked very hard at keeping up a front. It never mattered to anyone whether I passed or failed; now I had to make a decision. I had a struggle understanding math problems—not a good sign for a mechanical drawer. I was determined to seem okay even if I wasn't. Mostly, if you did not do well in school, you were labeled dumb or lazy, or a "problem." I wanted to avoid those labels. Mostly you were ignored. I was deeply hurt and harbored resentments when I was not allowed into the high school fraternity, "AAB," yet all my friends were. I tried to focus on the few successes that I had, yet the rejection that I felt ran deeper.

Post graduation from high school, I was really lost as to what I would do; boys and girls were fighting in Vietnam, others were protesting the war at home in America. I drank a lot of alcohol that summer, hung out with whoever would allow me to, and stayed on the fringes of groups. This was a time when I could have gone either way; I lacked mentoring. I am not blaming anyone for my alcoholism and drug addiction. Genetics have their way of trumping environment.

Summer jobs that year were a premium. Two of the most popular places to work for students were road or bridge construction and working at area camps. I did both. One camp experience that I think is humorous was one summer before I was old enough to work construction. Ray Jensen and I had ridden mini-Harleys, which were actually 50cc Harley Davidson mopeds, to Camp Sno-Hill in Lake Como every early morning from Hancock where we worked as maintenance help; we were grateful to have jobs. Basically I worked outside mowing grass and painting. My boss, the caretaker of the camp, was a man who was one step up from Neanderthal man and may have been the missing link. His name was Karl Dobish, commonly known as the "doobs" with a long O sound.

Karl was probably the filthiest person I had ever met, both in mind and body. He was short of stature, rotund, with a three-day beard every day, and he spoke through a Parodi cigar that never left his mouth except to bite off a piece and chew it. Karl could and would spit his foul saliva anywhere. Every word out of Karl's mouth was a swear word, and every sentence fragment that emanated from his perverted mind included "goddamit" and the word "fuck." Parodi cigars, themselves, are some of the foulest tasting to ever have a match put to them. They are made, I am sure, of dried dung from some remote foreign land that rejected the aged poop for fuel and mixed it with unknown floor sweepings, probably from a chicken coop. Karl proudly slept with one in his mouth.

One day Ray Jenson, who also worked doing about the same things I was doing, heard this squeal coming from under a bunk. This noise sounded like a cross between a human and a large animal that was distressed. Doobs had wedged himself under a bunkhouse where he was either peeking at girls who lived in the bunkhouse or fixing a leaking shower drain. Doobs was stuck. Ray and I looked at each other, and the grin on Ray's face said; "Leave him." We knew we could not, so we grabbed his legs and pulled him out. Karl still had the Parodi in his mouth and seemed visibly scared—and almost human for a change. He kept asking Ray and me if we thought he could have died from suffocation under the bunkhouse. We, of course, told him he was lucky we pulled him out, or he could have had a heart attack. Job security!

In the Hancock area, camps varied. Some were attended by upper-middle-class Jewish kids from New York City and surrounding suburbs, some camps had a religious mission, others an athletic program, and still others focused on arts and crafts, with drama and music as the core activities. These camps were usually eight weeks long, and the locals found employment either year-round as maintenance workers and caretakers or for the two months of summer as kitchen help and additional maintenance workers.

I saw that the relationship between the "locals" and "camp staff" broke out along cultural and social differences. The staff was made up of former campers or the counselors who directly stayed with and supervised the kids, and the people who did not work directly with the children were "hired help." I began working at Camp Starlight somewhere in the early seventies. I was hired as a dishwasher, Tom Keeley was the salad man, and Mike Silber was the head chef. Mike, a German, was raised in Berlin during World War II and had been professionally trained both as pastry chef and cook. Mike and I got along well, and over the years, his mentoring of my cooking skills took my abilities to a higher level.

We fed approximately six hundred folks three meals a day, cooking "kosher," which required strict separation of meat and dairy foods and separate kitchens, dishes, and tableware. Mike was a master at producing just the right amount of large quantities of food. I developed a strong sense of taste and smell. I discovered that some folks have it and some don't, and it was one of the rare talents I was blessed with. We worked together for over thirteen summers; sadly he died suddenly of a heart attack while visiting his sister in Berlin.

Some of my more memorable times were working construction with the Peake Brothers from Long Eddy, and J. R. Evanitsky on Route 206 from Trout Creek to Masonville, New York. This was my first construction job, and J. R. and I were constantly sent on errands that had no meaning, for sport. The evening usually ended at the bar in Masonville where drunkenness was expected and fighting was normal. J. R. and I had to drag Peakey out of the bar several nights a week just to get a ride home, as he was the chauffeur.

Bill Weisman, an insurance salesman from Liberty, New York, often came to the DI on business, and he took a liking to me. He must have seen something different in me, and he encouraged me to attend college. Since my SAT scores were not horrific, I had applied to some schools and been accepted at a few of them. Most were out of state and expensive. I was too shy in many ways to risk leaving home to go too far away.

This is where I got stuck. No one in my family went to college or knew what the process of the next step was. Even if they had this secret road map, they were too busy making a living to take the time to show me the way. Bill Weisman took the trouble to help me apply and get accepted at Sullivan County Community College in Fallsburg, New York, about forty miles east of Hancock. His opinion was that I should stay close to home until I got the rhythm of going to school; also, I would have guaranteed work at the Delaware Inn. Without his help, I would be packing groceries for a living—not that packing groceries is a bad thing; someone has to do it!

I believe that leaving my family as a young adult posed many issues. Learning how to say good-bye and how to leave the door open if I didn't succeed and needed to come back, and wanting to further their sense of pride in my success all played large in my plans. Again I lacked a map. What else was missing was feeling validated, being encouraged and supported by others to succeed.

Most of the academic problems I had struggled with in high school came with me to college. Ironically, the dormitory I was assigned to was another hotel, much larger and more glamorous than the one I was leaving. It was called the Green Acres, and it was about four miles out of Liberty, New York, near the towns of Woodbourne and Loch Sheldrake. The dormitory housed all guys. All the girls stayed at another hotel about ten miles away called the Olympic.

Understand these were "borscht belt" hotels that basically had customers on Jewish holidays or during the summer months; most of the business came from New York City. Being a college dorm in the off-season was a bonus for them. The rooms were old in some of the sections of the hotel, and some additions were built in a more modern fashion. Some were suites; this meant that they had their own bathrooms. As college guys do, we drank beer, decorated our rooms with the empty cans, and cruised for chicks. Classes were held in prefabricated buildings in the town of South Fallsburg. For me, this was college. I liked the freedom that I had in making my own daily schedule, but the problem was that I didn't know how to manage my time. For the first few weekends, I went home, did not study, and lived in two different worlds. Transitions are very difficult for folks who have been traumatized or have learning disabilities.

Some of the professors could quickly see who was prepared and who wasn't. While I excelled in history, and some English courses, my major was accounting and business administration. After about four weeks, the accounting professor pulled me into his office and did me a favor; he suggested that I change my major to liberal arts, since accounting "was not my forte." Again, I had conceptual problems understanding the way accounting was organized. All I knew at that time was, "Thanks, Mr. Shambly."

Outside of class I was basically drinking, getting high, and hanging out. I was interested in music and could read history and literature for hours on end. In the end, I almost flunked out. Even I knew that getting thrown out of a community college was the bottom of the barrel. I had a hard time fitting in; I wasn't quite a hippie, I wasn't entirely against the war in Vietnam; I had friends and a brother there, and I did not like getting drunk and fighting as many of the rural male students did for sport. I was socially retarded. Each time I left Hancock there was a feeling of anxiety that was only managed with self-medication. Thank God for the sixties when an adequate supply was available!

On weekends I worked as a bellboy or carhop at various hotels in Sullivan County. Sometimes I would tend bar at a local ski resort, but the car hopping brought the best tips. On some weekends I would make $50 to $100 plus food and a small wage. By the next weekend, I was basically broke. My lifestyle was disorganized, and I knew little about managing money. Most of the wasted dollars went to buying others drinks and drugs, trying to buy friends.

Mostly the guys I knew drank and smoked pot or hash. Sometimes there would be other hallucinogens. Live music and black-lighted bars were the rage. Vanilla Fudge songs were in, and there was always a party somewhere. I thought that this was college life, but actually it simply was addiction at work. It's the disease that tells you that you don't have one.

On occasion I would go out on a date or come home and work and hang out in the bar at the D.I. I had little confidence and low esteem. The dates were usually for sex; I was good at taking hostages. But I did have a good "act as if" so I got by. Unfortunately the self-centered behavior was all about me; it was disingenuous, and you can only lie to yourself for so long.

After two years and an extra semester of focusing on drugs and ass, I finally got a degree in liberal arts. This was simply a degree that said you had better find a four-year college that will accept you if you ever want to qualify for a job.

During the following summer, I worked in Syracuse, New York, on Route 690 East, a road that was being built over the New York State Thruway at Baldwinsville. At the time, I was making at least $200 per week plus overtime. I had a sweet gig. On some weekends I went in for two hours to wet down the newly poured concrete slabs on the bridges and got paid for the day. A friend of my dad's from Deposit, New York, who was a superintendent for Savin Brothers Construction Company, gave me the job. I was broke every weekend. This was the first time that I became aware of blacking out from drinking.

One time I arrived in Hancock late at night, and in a blackout went to someone's house on the Cadosia/Apex road. I was told that it was about two in the morning when I knocked on the door. It seems the woman recognized me. I asked to use her bathroom, and then came out and lay down on her living room couch. These kind people woke me up for breakfast; I ate and left. All this was done in a blackout. Their son told me the story a couple of years later.

Chapter 17

ANOTHER TUTORIAL

I HEARD ABOUT A COLLEGE in the small city of Elmira, New York, that was changing their program from an all-female school to a coed campus. I applied to Elmira College and was accepted into their English/Secondary Education curriculum. Even with substandard grades, I was offered a work-study gig and a small reduction in tuition costs. I had never been west of Binghamton; however, I had few options. Apparently someone or something had my best interest at hand.

During my first year at Elmira, I was housed in an old Victorian house that had about seven bedrooms. There was one single room that had been the library, and it had its own bathroom and a soundproof door. Every guy wanted that room for obvious reasons. All the guys in McKenzie House were transfers and/or over twenty-one; we had no curfews and few rules. We all decided that whoever was the last "man" standing after drinking some swill made from five kinds of liquor would have the room and be the elected "resident advisor." I think that this guy named Jack fell over just before I did, and I was the winner of a private room and bath. There were 88 guys attending Elmira College that year and over 1100 girls and women on the campus. Yes, there was heaven for straight guys in the seventies.

By the time I graduated two years later, I had many girlfriends. One I became engaged to, a woman named Rosemary, who, after hanging with me for a while, left the ring on the dresser and ran away to California. All my relationships repeated the same pattern: I wanted; I got; then I didn't want it or they did not want me. Each relationship had one common denominator—they were ethanol fortified.

What I failed to do was to attend classes; classroom settings were too intimate for me. I worked some weekends at the DI and during the week at the social security office in Elmira as part of my work-study. This money was not enough to supply my habits, so I stole money from the safe at the Delaware Inn. I had stooped to a new low, stealing from my family. I thought, on some level, if I could keep work or a mood-altering substance as a boundary between me and the rest of the world, I could manage. Apparently this plan was falling apart too.

I knew every bartender in the city of Elmira and never missed a party or a "happy hour." How I graduated and completed a student teacher internship as a high school English teacher is beyond me to this day. I liked the kids (most of them) where I student taught. Most of the teachers I found to be disinterested, yet I grew to love literature and books.

With my management of the dormitory, tragedies did occur. One Thanksgiving vacation evening, some local kid crashed one of the McKenzie parties and fell off a balcony to his death. Someone put a blanket over him, and soon the police were combing the place for evidence of foul play. By 3 a.m., the body was gone and the party rolled on. No one in the dorm knew his name. I was put on probation for a while as I was supposedly in charge of the house.

Often at these times, the devil and angel would visit me on opposing shoulders. On one shoulder, I knew that there should not be any nonstudents in the house since it was Thanksgiving vacation and the only folks who should be there that time of night would be the residents or their registered guests. On the other shoulder sat the devil who said "fuck it," enjoy yourself and have a good time. I was with a young woman named Bonnie, who was not supposed to be in my room at that time either. In the end, I was just plain scared of the consequences and opted to tell the truth about the untoward visitors. The college administration seemed more concerned about the girl in the room than the guy who fell to his death. Values change slowly; we should all wear mirrors around our necks.

Somewhere in the second semester of my junior year, I hit on this young woman who was more serious about a relationship than I was. I met her at the Eagle Hotel, which was very similar to the Delaware Inn. The occasion was a birthday party some of my friends held for me. It was sometime in March. I do not remember driving from Hancock to Elmira that Saturday; I had washed down some quaaludes with beer and was totally crashed when I arrived there. I also had a bottle of terpin hydrate with codeine as a kicker in my pocket. I remember having difficulty keeping my car on the road.

The next day I had forgotten about our liaison; however, LuLu did not. LuLu expected us to be at least friends. LuLu was smart; she lived on the good side of the tracks. I didn't have the esteem or the conscience at that time to have a normal college girlfriend. After the usual on-again, off-again, in what I remember as a sober conversation about three months later, she asked me if I was an alcoholic.

LuLu was from a part of New Jersey where I imagine that her high school health class went beyond my learning about Mr. Tooth from Ms. McKernan at Hancock Central. Her high school apparently offered more education about alcoholism and drug addiction. I was appalled and also embarrassed that she asked that question of me, yet there was something inside of me that knew LuLu was on to something. There was some truth to her message. I have never forgotten that conversation. Today I am sorry that I hurt her feelings; back then it didn't matter. If I was an alcoholic, so was everyone else I knew from home and hung with at college. I left Elmira in May of 1972 with a diploma and a growing sense that once again I had been a failure.

Chapter 18

Back at the Inn

THE INN WAS A WORLD unto itself, and there were many places needing exploration beyond the first two floors. I was awed by the construction of the building and its stature. I could not find out who built the inn, but whoever did was talented enough to build upward. There were three floors atop the ground floor that all had twelve-foot ceilings. The outside of the inn was covered with a fiberboard that probably had some asbestos in its makeup. In the future, I would put aluminum siding on the building with a layer of rigid insulation. The roofs were peaked and there were two large chimneys made of unlined brick.

Under the main staircase was a closet that held a safe and the readily needed bar supplies. There was a dining room door that led into a smaller dining area off the main room. The rooms were separated by another inoperative fireplace with a decorative mantel and firebox cover. The tables were a combination of round and square, dressed with white tablecloths and surrounded by wooden chairs. These were reset each evening to be appropriate for the time of the year and the day of the week. On weekends, the bar crowd would spill over into the dining area. During holidays, the bottom floor would be decorated, and the tablecloth colors would match the season.

The adjacent bar was a horseshoe with about twenty-five stools. There was a rounded beer cooler at one end and ice and draft beer taps on one side. Later on I would modernize the draft beer system and put a direct draw system that used a walk-in cooler in a new addition adjacent to the new kitchen. This would allow beer taps on both sides of the bar and more selections of draft beer. Also in the barroom were a pool table, a jukebox, and two cigarette machines (cigarettes cost fifty cents at that time). All three were very busy.

The windows throughout the building were large, six-foot double-cased monsters that had mostly been painted shut over the years. All the ceilings were tall and needed some refurbishing because the plaster had suffered from moisture, vibration from the trains passing, and yellowing from cigarette smoke.

You could enter the bar from the dining room or the lobby or from the east side of the building directly. Most often, the interior door was used by the waitresses who bustled back and forth, bringing drinks to the diners from the barroom. Straight through the kitchen and up the back stairs was a laundry facility and storage. There was a large laundry sink and cleaning supplies that were needed to wash and dry bedding, and to clean floors and windows. This was needed on a continuous basis. The kitchen and the floor above it were attached to the larger building, and future renovations that housed a new kitchen and barroom storage would remove them.

The first large room upstairs in the main building was called the "Rotary Room" because the Rotary club met there every week. They were the business gentry of Hancock who met weekly and complained more about the food and the cost of their weekly luncheon than any diners we had. Sometimes I wondered if that was their reason for grouping. These mostly middle-aged white males would vote to go somewhere else for their meeting and lunch and soon, being dissatisfied with the fare there, would come back to the inn.

Individually, the members of the Rotary club were the commerce folks that supported this small village. Many of them were very successful business people and were relatively wealthy. Sadly they bickered a lot among themselves, and those who were leaders had little following. This indicated to me that as a group they had little interest in the larger community, or if they did, they could never get beyond the annual spaghetti supper to provide the leadership needed to help Hancock grow with the changing times. This room would also be majorly renovated in the later years after I bought the inn.

On the floor where I lived, two flights up from the lobby, there were eleven rooms and a hall bath. While the windows were large and let in plenty of light, the tallness of the rooms made it seem darker. Some of the walls and ceilings were cracked from the train vibrating the building several times a day. It seemed that the vibrations were most damaging to the rooms on this floor.

The entire building was constructed of lath-and-plaster walls and ceilings, which was the standard long before Sheetrock and tape. The laths were these thin, perhaps two inches wide by a quarter inch thick, slats that varied in length; they were usually about two to three feet long. I imagine that they were made of pine or hemlock, some soft wood for sure. They would be nailed to the studs to form a surface for the plaster. Craftsman would then plaster over this wood structure to make the wall. Sometimes there would be pieces of netting or a mesh made of various materials that helped support the plaster. In the end, this type of construction contributed to the buildings' rapid demise by fire. The spaces between the studs were without fire blocks, and this made for a natural ductwork that the fire could follow.

The fourth floor was really an open attic that had been built out with the square footage of an average house. There were three large bedrooms, a kitchen, and a very large living room. You could enter the remaining part of the attic that was not part of the living area and see the construction of the roof; which was quite spectacular. The unlined chimneys were brick and mortar and needed patching or a liner installed to make them safe for wood or coal use. There were cleanouts in the attic that allowed access to the chimney from the place where they went through the roof. That was an important point where any wood that was burned would create creosote with the temperature differences inside the attic and outside above the roofline.

By the time I finished two years of college, my grandparents (Dad's mom and stepfather) were living on this floor and had renovated much of it. My parents bought a small house in town, and whenever I was home, I had a room in the inn for a while until I moved on. Certainly this changed my feelings toward my family. I really felt as if I had left them or they had left me. I felt alone, yet I had little desire to not move on. This to some extent seems usual for most young adults, especially during the sixties and seventies.

The basement, or cellar, of the hotel was one of my favorite places in the building; it felt like I was in the guts of a large machine. There were five large areas, all with stone floors and brick walls. This was a great place to have a workshop, and my grandfather set up his Lionel train set to replicate a railroad yard in the largest room. Grandpa Dietz had been an engineer on the D&H Railroad for forty years, and he could not give it up. I don't know how he navigated all the steps up and down, as at one time he weighed over three hundred pounds.

There was a beer cooler in the basement where the keg beer was kept and tapped. This system was an older cork-and-ram system that took some getting used to whenever a keg needed changing in a hurry. You had to run down to the cellar and untap one keg and tap another. The smell of yeast and hops was strong there as beer shot out in small amounts whenever a keg was tapped.

During this time, in New York state you could legally serve, buy, and drink beer, wine, or whiskey at eighteen years of age. Folks were going to war these years in Vietnam, and this was often the argument for keeping the drinking age the same as the draft age—eighteen.

I believe that I envisioned myself being part of the inn and also having the freedom to leave at times. The inn had a way of drifting into one's DNA. The bar was busy from opening at 10 a.m. until closing, usually at 2 or 3 a.m., and the kitchen was kept busy. These were the times that construction on the highway (Route 17) was at its peak and business was at its most profitable. I helped out wherever I was needed but also had a desire to experience other jobs too.

Chapter 19

The Initiation

After graduation from college, I found few jobs for English teachers. At the Delaware Inn, I was asked to bartend some evenings and Sunday afternoons. My first encounter with some of the local legends was with this large man named D. who ran a garage next door. He became irate because I did not draw the proper amount of draft beer to back up his shot of Christian Brothers Brandy. D. was unpredictable, and I didn't like that he thought he could come in the bar and grab me and threaten me over a glass of beer. The next day he apologized and was a totally different guy. Regardless of his temperament, he was the type of hard-working blue-collar guy who came to the inn during the daytime shift. There was a guy named Billy from around Roscoe who cut logs or stone for a living and sometimes stayed in Hancock. He was my first customer most Sundays and would order seven shots of Seagram's 7 whiskey and seven aspirin. Within three to four minutes, he had finished them all. Then he could start drinking normally again.

Many of the customers would stop in at the same time each day, and they liked the bartender knowing just what they wanted.

Some suffered from some stage of alcoholism, I now believe. The more I tended bar, the more I could rationalize that my drinking was far less. It was a useful ruse.

Much of the activity until lunchtime surrounded the pool table, which the bar manager, Clarkie, ruled over. Many a sucker was pulled in by him and then he would get serious. Oralls turned out to be a good pool player too; he shot a much rougher game though. Lunchtime was a mix of folks in the bar and dining room; the food was home cooking, good and reasonably priced. At that time, Annie Dibble ran the dining room and did it well. I can visualize her backing out of the kitchen door into the dining room with a handful of plates full of "specials" and telling the cooks what to have ready next for the dining room and to take care of the bar orders. Annie had the ability to move quickly, not waste any steps, and handle a large number of people who sometimes were demanding.

After work, the construction guys came in. Although Clarkie resented being helped, sometimes he did need it as these guys had voracious appetites for their favorite drinks. I knew one guy, Tommy, who was a couple of years older than I was. Tommy worked on road construction running equipment. He was a regular and could easily win the "world's fastest drinking screwdrivers contest." Many of these folks were not problematic, just the salt of the earth living the dream. Rewarding oneself at the end of a day's work seemed normal. Occasionally we would get an argument between construction workers; usually one bought the other a drink and the discussion evaporated. By shift change at 6 p.m., most of the guys had gone home, or if they lived at the hotel would have gone up to their rooms. It would be rare that any women were there at that time of the day, unless it was a Friday afternoon.

The night brought out the younger crowd, and many were just "kids in training" while others were simply moving through that single time of their lives and would go on to be "normies"—what those of us with alcoholism called normal drinkers. There were some who reacted violently to whatever they were drinking and came into the bar to start fights. Most of those guys did not have a clue as to how alcohol and other drugs affected them. There were about two or three guys that you just did not want to drink at your bar; sociopathic behavior mixed with ethanol often equals psychopathy. Being barred from drinking at someone's establishment, in Hancock, was akin to being branded. I think we grew up watching too many westerns.

I spent the next year working at the Treadway Inn on Route 17, the west side of Vestal, New York, in a small village named Owego. I was naturally attracted to cooking, and still there were no available teaching jobs in the early seventies in my home area except substitute teaching. I learned a lot about cooking there, especially about soups and sauces from a guy named Nick, who was professionally trained. As always, there is drama in the restaurant business and me being me, I could not stay away from the action. While there, I had another relationship with a young woman who worked at the restaurant. In the end, my pattern of behavior repeated itself. I became disgruntled, and the relationship ended when I left for Florida to escape from any emotional consequences once again.

At that time, my brother Gerry wanted to go to Florida too. He had done a short stint at a community college somewhere in New York state and partied his way into suspension. We planned on going to Miami since the job market in that area, at that time, was hot. We first went to Coral Gables. That area of Miami and the adjoining community of Coconut Grove were becoming popular. It was a hip time, but our budget had other realities, and we ended up south of there in an area that was more transient called Kendall. We had to keep watch each night to protect our car from having the tires stolen and the entire car being stripped. I decided if I parked in front of the apartment, my car would be more visible and in less danger. The thieves were slick; they only stole the outside wheels and tires that were away from our apartment house. They left that side of the vehicle up on concrete blocks. I was stunned. Welcome to the world Dan, I told myself, yet emotionally, I was a very immature young man who was filled with rage. We were a couple of hicks making our way in the city.

Both Gerry and I landed cooking jobs at the same restaurant, called the Original Pub. This was one of three larger restaurants owned in the area by Longchamps Corp., a restaurant company from New York. The restaurant was on Coral Way in upscale Coral Gables and was popular for its steak house decor, the quality of its meat, and live charcoal grilling. I worked in the kitchen and Gerry worked out on the live charcoal hearths. There was a great mix of folks who worked there. One was Pantera, a left-handed fry cook who drank whiskey about every fifteen minutes from his locker in the cooks' bathroom—a hole in the wall where rats were common. Pedro, a former airplane mechanic from Cuba, was a runner. He would tell us that in Cuba he was a "gigolo." Pedro's job was to coordinate food from the back kitchen and the front hearths. He was responsible for getting everyone's food at the same time to the same table.

We had a butcher, an Italian guy who had emphysema and chain-smoked. He kept the meat cooler rotated because all our meat was prime and aged. When a steak was ordered, he would cut whatever size and cut you wanted. The manager was a guy named Elliot; he was abusive and arrogant. Elliot was also professional at being unfair. He was constantly in a rage and probably could have used some counseling and meds; who knew that then? One of the salad men, a Cuban who spoke little English, cut his hand badly one afternoon before the restaurant opened. No one seemed to care. I took him to the emergency department and got him stitched up; we were back in the restaurant within two hours. Elliot docked us both the two hours and threatened to fire me. I was surprised that no one killed Elliot.

Gerry had a terrific personality, and everyone loved working with him. I, on the other hand, was miserable and not liked. I felt entitled to the chef's job. My grandiose thinking was fueled by resentment and immaturity. The good times were working four tens and going to the Florida Keys for three days of diving. I loved this area of Florida, as it had not been overpopulated yet. You could camp on any of the many mini-islands for free. Again, I met this wonderful woman, Sue, yet could not get along with her. As usual, it was my sabotaging the relationship because she confronted me on my intimacy problems: "denial is not a river in Egypt." This behavior had turned into a pattern that would last many more years. Gerry ended up staying in Florida. In the future, my parents moved to the west coast of Florida near Clearwater, and Gerry moved to Safety Harbor, which was just across the Dale Mabry Bridge from Clearwater. He went to work for the same company that Dad and Mom worked for.

I headed back home, depressed and unhappy, and landed a teaching job at Hancock Central teaching English to high school sophomores. I also coached cross-country, a sport I had run in high school. Teaching in the school you graduated from, with teachers you had while you were a student there, is a disaster waiting to happen. My reputation was suspect. My homeroom assignment, room 214, was the former territory of Pat O'D. Just being there, in that room again, triggered a posttraumatic reaction; however, I had a great mentor and supervisor in Wellington Lester. He was a fantastic educator and administrator who worked hard to support us newer teachers.

In those days, men teachers and women teachers had their

own lounges; smoking was encouraged, and some of the teachers drank a lot (but few more than me). I was feeling like it was time to settle down and could see that the teacher's salary of $110 per week at that time was starvation wages. After all, didn't anyone know that I had arrived? After my second year of teaching, I resigned. I could have stayed and would have been given a tenured position; however, my grandiose thinking was at work again. I had no problem finding resentments to justify my leaving.

I began dating Roxanne K., a good friend of my brother Gerry. Roxie was smart, beautiful, and a hard worker. I knew her family, and we dated her senior year while she went to Wilkes College. I am not sure what she thought about some of my bizarre behavior, but she married me. We had the wedding reception at Camp Starlight where I had worked that summer. Roxanne taught high school English for one year. There were some changing politics in the administration at Hancock Central, and the Board of Education hired an administrator who clearly had issues with young women teaching. Roxanne left her job there. I believe she was very hurt by this injustice, and we should have sued the school district. I probably did not take any action because this gave me plenty of justification to bitch, build resentments, and drink—my favorite pastimes.

I was a terrible husband, and in spite of having our first child, I would disappear, go on blackout binges, and have no accountability for myself. I do remember telling her that I had a problem with alcohol. She wisely responded; "It's your problem." This was a hard statement to hear at that time.

I wanted to buy the Delaware Inn from my parents. This of course would solve all my problems, I thought. At that time, there were loans available from the Small Business Administration, yet I had little credit history. In spite of all this, I was determined to buy the inn. Stu Goff ran the bank. He was the father of Buzzy, who had split to Canada with me several years before. My parents were worn out and wanted to sell at a fair price; however, they did not want to be financially involved or hold a mortgage. Larry and Rose Simpson, friends of ours, were also looking for a business opportunity at that time. Along with Roxanne and me, with the help of David Drum, a Marine Midland banker, we obtained a small business loan. When the local bank saw we were serious and could raise the money to buy the inn, they became more user friendly. After all, at this time the inn was a major source of cash flow in the community and the bank. Hancock Bank did not want to lose that business. After much negotiating, the four of us bought the Delaware Inn.

We divided up the duties; Roxanne ran the dining room and the catering arrangements, I did the cooking, Rosie did the books, and Larry ran the bar. We had our issues but did very well that first year. We all took vacations and had a profitable year. Roxanne and I went to Spain to see Mike Silber for a vacation, and Larry and Rosie went to Curacao.

We were on top of the world, and business was growing rapidly. Then something changed. I think it was a little over one year into the partnership when Larry and Rosie said they "wanted out." I was no picnic to work with or for, and partnerships are like other relationships, something I was familiar with but not successful at. Larry and Rosie went on to buy Delaware Carting, and Roxie and I owned the inn. We had a daughter, Mercedes, and soon I was off and running again. Inside I was a sad and sick man; on the outside, I hid well among the bar customers. Roxie and I separated, and for a while I saw my future clearly and it was not pretty. We reconciled and had another daughter, Marne.

Again I was on a run, and this time I thought about suicide. I sought the help of a psychiatrist in Binghamton. After listening to my bullshit and con, he told me I had a problem with alcoholism, probably depression too, and it would get worse. He said that I may lose everything I had, including my family. Bingo; this was the second person who told me the truth. I decided to get a third opinion, but somewhere along the way I forgot to.

Mercedes and to a lesser extent Marne were raised in the Delaware Inn as young children. The employees were their surrogate parents. Clarkie and Charlie Rock retired, as did some of the other folks. Stanley Ansewitz, a Long Island transplant, ran the bar and the ordering. I hid in the kitchen, and in the summer worked at Camp Starlight. I worked hard and drank hard, as most of my customers did. In the world of "hospitality" this was not uncommon.

As the business grew, I took out a large loan and hired Clarkie and Doug Swartz to gut and renovate the floor above the barroom to make a catering facility. Additional improvements were made to the dining area, and I had put in a new kitchen and storage room. The upstairs guest rooms were no longer viable, and the food and beverage business along with the catering trade was growing faster than I could keep up with it.

I hired a chef, Nino, and the two of us worked well together and continued to grow the food business. The saboteur reappeared; the pattern grew more severe. I could not stand success. This time I believed that I had fallen love with still another woman, and another, and another, and my marriage with Roxanne was over.

During this time, articles in several widely accepted magazines were extolling the miracles of a white powder that came from the coca leaf grown in South America. It was said that the stimulant effect of this "drug" was not addictive and held promise in the medicinal field. It promised increased energy and concentration. My response was, "Perfect." This wonder drug would help me be more, do more, and unknown to the authors of these promotional articles, drink more. It was not long before my associates and I were snorting large amounts of this miracle drug, cocaine, and drinking more and longer. I had crossed a line for sure and was an addict as well as an alcoholic.

I didn't believe that the street was "dead-ended" for me. Somehow I thought I could figure it out. My three favorite self-lies were, *I am different; I can control it;* and *It won't happen to me.* Cocaine mixed with alcohol has a synergistic effect, and it was cyclic for me. My first feeling always seemed to be anxiety, especially if I was in an "I can quit whenever I want to" mood. It was hardest saying, "I will stop" and then shortly finding myself in the same cyclic pattern all over again. The anxiety usually ended when I started drinking, and the drinking usually led to drugging. I would medicate, and as soon as I stopped, depression would follow; then the anxiety would begin again. Self-medication was not working very well, and I became somewhat manic at times. There were binge trips to New York, and affairs with an odd assortment of women. I bought and renovated a cottage on the river, took flying lessons, and bought an airplane I rarely flew. I liked expensive cars and bought and sold several properties in a short time. Then these material things all disappeared, mostly up my nose and down my throat. My insight and my judgment were becoming more suspect.

Deprivation as a child is traumatic too; I often rationalized that as the motivator for acute dervish and manic behavior. I guessed that as an adult, the shame of poverty can drive you in many different directions; some folks become misers, I pissed it away.

Chapter 20

A ROAD WELL TRAVELED

SEDUCTION ALWAYS PRECEDES ABUSE. MOST habits can seem wearisome; it's a ruse. The habit simply plays out the script you have agreed upon. Most folks figure it out too late: the habit maims or kills before you recognize that intended friendships now are deadly enemies. It's like the proverbial scorpion who asks the frog for a ride across the creek; it is inevitable that the frog will get stung. There were times when I saw this clearly. I had been forewarned twice, yet my denial was deeply rooted in my survival skills, and the truth came wrapped in deception. Self-deception is the most powerful lie. Once you take your hand off the chess piece, the move is over.

Now it was happening more often. I was seeing the clear picture and could not keep up with the images or thoughts. I would get angry over things that used to be nothing. My lack of self- tolerance was often visited on others. I couldn't handle making mistakes or being wronged; I projected this on anyone else around me. It was all criticism to me. To admit mistakes felt very self-demeaning. On a deeper level, it felt like rejection or abandonment. I needed to be able to trust to make mistakes. Control is an illusion; yet it is one of the few we cling to. That was on the inside. What I did see in others was that folks did not get very close to me for very long. What you thought of me was what I thought of me. When you liked me, I must be okay; when you didn't like me, I was shit. My inner self spent most days raging.

Life on the outside appeared good. I tried to take advantage of the normal things in my life. In the afternoon I would play golf. In season I hunted deer or fished. I had taken up distance running, which was fashionable. I had quit smoking cigarettes about five years before, and of course, had another new last-est and best-est girlfriend. I became active in the local chamber of commerce. Half of me liked my life.

In a manic state I was getting busy again. I bought an interest in a bar in Delhi with Bruce Piesecki; that scene was too crazy for me. After snorting coke and drinking, I almost got killed one late night on the way home when a truck ran over my car as I stopped for the stop sign that intersected the Apex road with the Cannonsville Dam road. I ran from that deal. Once I woke up at Three Mile Island with a woman in my bed and a large bag of pot and beer bottles all around us. How did I get there? Another time I awoke on the Peas Eddy Road, truck parked, me sleeping on the ground about ten feet from the water near Eel Wire Hollow. I no longer knew what normal was—apparently I cared less. The downward spiral continued.

One late winter, perhaps an early spring day, I was sitting in the lobby of the inn reading the *Hancock Herald*. The welcome sun brought the promise of longer days through large windows that faced south. Few trains were running across the street, and the tracks were becoming less obvious as time went by. The chimneys of houses near the river were curling up a damped down gray smoke that indicated warmer days coming. There was a hot fire in the lobby wood stove, and I liked the warmth of it all. I needed a friend.

All of a sudden from nowhere a wiry man with an orange knit cap came whooping into the lobby shouting, "Heh baby!" His hair was mussed; he had some growth that could pass for whiskers on his stout chin. He was dressed in blue jeans that were rolled up to accommodate his leg length, and a green sweatshirt that appeared to be a third layer of clothing that clung tightly to his muscular frame. In his mouth was a short cigar (I believe unlit). This was my first real introduction to Coon Hill Johnny. Johnny was a walker—actually, a fast-paced walker who often carried a thirty-five-pound bag of dog food on his shoulder as he made the trek back from Hancock to Coon Hill and his family of dogs. Johnny belonged to the village of Hancock and the surrounding hamlets the same way the river did. He was as much a part of the locale to those of us who lived there as anyone. If I could paint a picture of Hancock, Coon Hill Johnny would be in it.

Occasionally Johnny would stop for a cup of coffee, a shot of Old Grand-Dad Bourbon, or just to yak about the latest sports news. He had little money. Most of the work that Johnny did was either for charity or an occasional barter. His goal each day was to bring sunshine into folks' lives. He would visit you if you were sick, and if you needed something fixed, he would help. When I didn't see him for a while, I often wondered how he was and what he was up to.

One winter it was very cold, and Johnny had no money for fuel. Dibble, who was Annie the waitress's husband and the town justice at that time, did his best to help him. Johnny could be prideful, and this of course worked against his best interest. I convinced him to stay at the inn for a couple of weeks until it warmed a bit; but then he was off, half running as if he was late for something only he knew of.

You could tell the season of the year by Johnny's clothing. In the colder season and into spring, he wore a signature orange skullcap, a red handkerchief around his neck, and several layers of hand-me-down shirts and jackets. One Christmas I bought him a Carhartt heavy-duty insulated coverall and some insulated boots. In the next month, he had given them away and/or traded for some used winter clothes. When summer came, he would wear the same work boots that he wore other seasons but would sometimes wear denim shorts, and over the course of the next few months, he would get a very brown tan. Johnny seemed to prefer green T-shirts as he often had one on. His facial hair would grow with the cooling weather of the fall, and by spring, his hair and beard were full. Sometimes at Christmas he would wear a Santa hat and with his full beard and hair, he could fool most kids.

As Johnny aged, he had heart problems. I believe that he had a pacemaker after several heart attacks. Alcohol abused Johnny more than he abused alcohol; it was an occasional hoot for him but nothing serious. He liked cigars, yet I cannot remember him ever having one lit; he basically munched on them. Johnny had a very low tolerance for excess. As with the rest of his life, he was a minimalist. He was a devout Catholic. This contributed to his piousness and was sometime misinterpreted; I think that he was always praying. Later on in life, he had several strokes. The last time I was in Hancock I visited him on his deathbed. There appeared to be stroke damage and some dementia, yet we did connect for a few minutes and we were very happy to see each other and laugh about good times. Johnny was the same with me whether I was in a good mood or not. He taught me the basic levels of trust and an important lesson: to thine own self be true.

I had another friend who came to Hancock from New York City at about the same time that I bought the Delaware Inn. His name was Alex Conte, and he and his wife, Sigrid, ran the LaSalette restaurant located on the Hancock golf course. Alex was Italian and also fluent in French, with a New York accent; he was always a gentleman. Mechanical things intrigued Alex, as they did me, and we were soon good friends. We both saw our interests in food and hospitality as being complementary and not competitive. I shared anything I could with him and he did the same with me. Alex's ability to overcome most obstacles, whether personal, business, family, or just when we had bad luck at hunting, with his spiritual philosophy that God was in charge always impressed me.

Alex and Sigrid had many children, and the beauty of Sigrid shown in the girls and the courage of Alex in his sons. We hunted together, made sausage from pigs and deer meat, and went shopping for things we did not need in Scranton and other less-known places. We talked about everything. There was a sense of normal about Alex, and unlike me, he seemed comfortable in his own skin. Everywhere Alex went he made friends, and this was an eye-opener for me—that I could make friends and not have a manipulative agenda; that no one had to take advantage of another or have to have the upper hand. These are second-grade social skills that I missed. Sigrid died a year or two ago, and Alex is retired and has fought cancer to a standstill as of our last conversation.

Alex also brought a chef with him when he came from New York, where his mother owned a restaurant. Nino was his name. When he grew older and Alex needed him less at the restaurant, Nino came to work for me at the inn. He was a good man with many skills that made sense to me at that time in the kitchen. Nino was Italian, born near the Yugoslav border. This made for some interesting recipes and various ways to prepare new dishes for me. Today he is retired and lives in Hancock. Alex and Nino traveled to Italy and visited relatives a few years ago. What a rich gift to Hancock they are.

Chapter 21

THE FORK IN THE ROAD

"Gone tomorrow, here today, just in case you got
something to say."
(Allison Krauss)

FOR SOME REASON KNOWN ONLY to addicts in recovery and other non–flat earth society folks, there seems to be a point where change becomes inevitable. My nights were filled with praying, while puking in homage to the ivory god in the bathroom. My days were filled with anxiety, and in spite of the many times I told myself that I could stop drinking, I did not. Then there were the folks I avoided—the bar zombies—whose numbers multiplied. The younger and older, they reminded me of what I was, what I was becoming. I walked with my head down, avoiding anyone who looked me in the eye or wanted to engage with me.

Something was changing. I was not in control of this change, and I seriously considered taking the .38 special from under my truck seat and eating it. I could feel myself splitting apart. I was whoever anyone wanted me to be at that moment. All sense of who I was became hidden to me. The main street drug for me was cocaine, chased with alcohol. I remember pledging to not drink, and then within one or two days, or sometimes only hours, I was again rationalizing why it was okay. Once I drank, all bets were off; cocaine was just dessert.

Sometime in 1985 after twenty years of research and development with my addictions, it was time to possibly consider self-defeat. My drinking progressed—how could it not?—because I had an endless supply and answered to no one. I could be one of the guys on the outside and engage in many of the normal activities of everyday life. I made adjustments that I thought would help. The problem was me. Switching drinks, drinking light beer, not drinking for three days, no drugs, praying, only drinking wine, and various other schemes always landed me back at "go," without the "get out of jail free" card.

There were a few good folks in my life at this time; a slight shift occurred in my ability to see them. Not that anyone else was bad. This was just my perception since I was playing on both sides of the fence. I was single and had given the inn to Roxanne, and within a month she had given it back to me. Perhaps this was the bottom. I could only hope that the elevator couldn't go down any further.

Whenever I came down from my anxiety attacks, which was usually after sleeping in the afternoon, there were moments of clarity. This was unplowed ground for me, yet it was a clearing. For a brief minute or two, I knew that I had to make some choices, and pretty soon. As coincidence would have it, I ran into a young woman who I knew from high school, Kathy Mattice. I accepted an invitation from her to go to Florence Vitale's home one evening a week to participate in a "group" or possibly it was a "prayer group." In either case, I wouldn't have known the difference anyway. The group was basically Catholic in members; however, it was not the usual script. We did some praying and talking about spiritual needs and the needs of the community at large. This somehow stuck with me. Here was this group of folks who had no agenda, were not making me attend, and were friendly—and most of all, it seemed that they liked me in spite of my self-loathing. They were interested in others besides themselves.

My egocentric self wanted to be right on top of any action, of course, and Kathy in her wisdom gave me an assignment to keep me busy. She asked me to feed some hungry folks who had little resources or social support that lived nearby. This couple lived in a shack and parked their old car in part of the house. I believe that the kitchen floor that adjoined the garage area floor was dirt.

So I did. At first I would leave food outside their shack because they would not answer the door. In a short amount of time, perhaps a couple of weeks, I was able to speak with these folks. It turned out that I knew a child of theirs, or at least a niece (I can't remember which). The point was that I had surrendered a small part of myself to someone and or something else, and for a moment was not feeding my insatiable appetite for attention, control, and/or mood alteration. In my mind, I thought I was magnanimous for this simple gesture; little did I know I was really serving myself.

Another thing that "happened" at about the same time was that I was asked to teach English to some children who were living on what amounted to a commune in French Woods. Folks who owned a local business franchise in town had converted a ranch house and a trailer into space for some young adults, and at times teens, who were staying there. I didn't get why they were there at first; I had never heard of them before and certainly did not know what "recovery" was. I was there because I felt important—needed and valued. At that time, I was simply trying to impress others. To my recollection, one of the owners was a recovering alcoholic who had been sober some twenty years at that time and was looking to help others, including families and teens, to stop drinking through Alcoholics Anonymous and Al-Anon. I had never heard of such groups, did not know what alcoholism was, nor was I really interested. I was just interested in someone liking and wanting me around, and in feeling appreciated as a teacher for the kids there. I also knew that if I kept living my life the same way, I would keep ending up where I had been.

The apparent history was that there had been a "recovery commune" called East Ridge in Hankins, New York that these folks were associated with. As groups often do after they outgrow themselves, they spawn other groups. The place was named the Family, later known as the Family Foundation School. The children there were required to have some schooling, and the foundation needed some legitimacy as a business. Others and I volunteered our services at the Family. I was later paid for providing counseling to the school-age children who stayed there.

About noon during one of the days there, a meeting was called, and everyone went into the cramped cellar dining area for what was described as an "AA meeting." What I heard was not what I expected. An opening was read from a book, and the Twelve Steps were read. Then Twelve Traditions were read. I was trying to stay respectful, but in my mind I was waiting for the secret handshake and someone asking for money. No one did. Then a section was read that was called the Promises; this section rocked me. I sat stunned as the words I heard interrupted my direction in life about one hundred eighty degrees. The misery and shame I felt about myself were in front of my face, but so was an out. I felt hope for the first time in what had been a very long time. The hair on my neck went up as the significance of those words became embedded in my brain. Could this be so?

If we are painstaking about this phase of our

development, we will be amazed before we are halfway through. We are going to know a new freedom and a new happiness. We will not regret the past nor wish to shut the door on it. We will comprehend the word *serenity* and we will know peace. No matter how far down the scale we have gone, we will see how our experience can benefit others. That feeling of uselessness and self-pity will disappear. We will lose interest in selfish things and gain interest in our fellows. Self-seeking will slip away. Our whole attitude and outlook upon life will change. Fear of people and of economic insecurity will leave us. We will intuitively know how to handle situations that used to baffle us. We will suddenly realize that God is doing for us what we could not do for ourselves. Are these extravagant promises? We think not. They are being fulfilled among us—sometimes quickly, sometimes slowly. They will always materialize if we work for them. (Alcoholics Anonymous, pp. 84–85)

Before I left there that day, I spoke with folks about what I had heard. I was wondering whether the whole crew that lived there were nuts, or I was psychotic or there was a trick up someone's sleeve. I had always professed a belief in a higher power that I usually called God. I had tried several different churches and denominations over the years. As a child, we were expected to attend religious instructions and prepare for the Catholic sacraments, we had no choice. Later on in life and after I was sober, I investigated several different religions. This did not feel like a religious setting or if it was, it reminded me of a Quaker meeting I had once attended where folks shared and related to each other. It certainly was about alcoholism and drug addiction, and I realized that these kids had the same battle with substances that I had. At the end of the meeting, we all held hands and said either the Serenity Prayer or the Lord's Prayer, I don't remember which, yet I felt no offense to the closing.

Two hours had passed at the meeting, and I was still talking with two strangers about this shit called my life. I asked about these "promises" and how long it took for them to become real for me. I wanted a timeline. They laughed. Then one of them said to me, "We have been talking for some time now. Have you thought about drinking?" I hadn't. They then asked me if I would not take a drink today, and said we could talk some more tomorrow. I had wanted to stop drinking for so long, but could not, that I doubted myself. I told them that I would not drink the rest of that day or night. The important idea that came to me was that I now had made a decision to *not* take a drink. It was an option I hadn't realized that I had since I was fifteen.

That night was painful. I owned a bar and a restaurant, and everyone I knew was drinking. What would I do with my life? I cried, I prayed, I threw up, and I had nightmares. I was caught; both of me had sat down and made a decision and a promise. The internal struggle between the Dan who wanted to drink and the Dan who wanted to not drink fought it out. I made it through the night. I did not drink alcohol or take any drugs except some Motrin. I did it again the next day too, and the next night and the next day. I was not drinking, and I was able to not drink for thirty, sixty, and then ninety days.

I kept it a secret from everyone at the inn. Later on I realized that no one really cared about my drinking; it was my problem. The only ones who knew my dilemma were a few of the guys that I liked at the place in French Woods. One guy was quite an orator. When he spoke about his addiction, he was telling about mine too. Many of the guys there were younger than me, and I related to what they were going through. They did not know it, but having others who thought and felt the same way that I did helped me with my feelings of thinking that I was a uniquely horrible person. I had been living with the notion that if I told you what I thought, felt, and did, you would certainly reject me. I would be a reject, something I had been trying to come to terms with my whole life.

For the next six months I did not drink. I told some of the folks at the inn and stepped back from the business of running the bar. I gave more responsibility to my employees; I think I said the Serenity Prayer over three thousand times each month.

Then at six months, the bottom dropped out. I have never felt the blackness and despair I felt then. I could hardly move physically, and my head was full of fog. I was a numb zombie. The recovery word for this state is *mocus*; psychiatry calls it major depressive disorder. Was this really worth it? I wanted to be "normal" like all the other folks I knew. They drank and were happy; some drugged and seemed to like it. How would I golf? What would I tell people? What about wine? Would women like me? The oddest thoughts surfaced. Can I drive safely? How will I sleep? Who will take care of my daughters? How could I run my business or leave the business; then what would I do? I felt tremendous guilt for my failed marriage and my outrageous behavior. If only I could get back to some point in time and erase the damage done. So, I had not had a drink for six months, yet I was far from sober. Not drinking did not guarantee that everything would go well in life; in fact, not drinking exposed much of what had been going on for a long time in my head and in my behavior. There were deeper issues that the drugging and drinking medicated. As usual, in my case, drinking and drugging were only symbolic of deeper issues, yet they became their own problems.

Roxanne and I had been separated and agreed to go to a weekly "encounter" group for couples and some single divorced folks who lived at the Family. Tony and Betty, the founders of the Family usually facilitated the group; however, sometimes folks from East Ridge were there and also participated or led the group. There were few guidelines: you could not leave your seat, and you could not "rat-pack" or gang up on another person. Usually there was time for one or two folks to "run or talk" about their issues, and then the group would confront their denial. I loved the verbal battles. I was in deep denial, and emotionally, this reminded me of times when I was a child and our family was crazy and everyone was fighting. Some of these people turned out to be good facilitators, some not.

In many ways the group was a cluster fuck, except what came out of it for me was an agreement with Roxanne that I would not drink or drug. I would attend AA, and I would get a "sponsor," someone in the AA program who knew the steps and was a good mentor. At the end of one year, we would talk about reconciliation. Roxanne would attend Al-Anon and get a sponsor from that group.

At the end of the year, my behavior had not really changed much. I still had girlfriends, I was scared of commitment, I always wanted the exit light on. I wanted to try reconciliation, but I was nowhere near ready. Roxanne said, "No, not again." She was exploring a relationship with someone else in the group. This stunned me. *She doesn't want me?* I thought. It is a sick commentary that someone finally gets rid of you after you were the one responsible for years of lying, cheating, and stealing. Now I was jealous. Some are sicker than others, and it took five years of recovery to figure out it was me who was one of those who was "sicker than others."

I played the victim. I had been rejected, and self-pity and

depression increased my desire to drink. Either out of rebellion or resentment, or out of some core issue of my childhood, or just because I wanted to be in control, I was at the point of saying, "fuck it all." I had not had any alcohol for over a year, but I was not sober; I was "emotionally drunk"!

Some of the saddest stories that came out of the Family Foundation during that time were the matchmaking that was done there. Dating was encouraged at times when residents were early in their recovery, and emotionally and physically most vulnerable. Many of the young people who came there to find recovery ended up married to each other as a result of this influence. I believe it was Tony's way of rationalizing others' unresolved conflicts with his own marriage, children, or family. Intimate physical relationships are often lethal in early recovery, but one could not have stopped some folks from eventually getting together and marrying, or from dating each other away from the facility. It would not surprise me if many of the folks that came together there are now estranged and or have had relapses to alcohol or drugs.

When the Family Foundation moved to the large farm they purchased a few miles down the road from the original location, the facility and philosophy of the Family became overwhelmingly Catholic. A priest by the name of Father A. taught religion classes and held masses there regularly. Management wanted a chapel and built one in the main building. Father A. was a nice guy; however, he did not understand that some folks don't want to convert to Catholicism. Like many religious folks, he often missed the point that alcoholism and addiction are diseases. Another example of this misunderstanding surfaced when the priest from St. Paul's Church, named Father David, petitioned the diocese to annul my marriage to Roxanne. I could see through that, as Roxanne worked for the church at that time. She wanted a clean slate to get remarried to a recovering resident of the Family. I couldn't blame her. I was the lout, but I questioned the church's rationale. Father David had little to offer; he was not a nice man.

At times management of the Family espoused some hybrid of a philosophy—basically, whatever benefited the organization at the time. Tony wanted to have a profitable business, and that was his main focus. Betty was more enlightened and understood the struggle that quitting alcohol is. There were many conflicts about the direction the Family would take in the future. In my opinion, they became a "private school," because there was the least amount of oversight from any governing agency, and they had found a funding source to pay for the "students" that were sent there— taxpayer dollars. The original intent of the Family was a beautiful thing, but as usual, commercialism eventually eats its own.

Soon there were AA meetings in Hancock at the Catholic church hall. This was started by a group of newly sober folks, mainly a woman named Brenda. After that there were meetings found in Deposit, Walton, and of course, many in Binghamton, New York.

I had spoken with both my parents about my marital situation, some of my behaviors, and that I believed that I was an alcoholic who needed help. Dad was supportive and helpful; Mom took it personally and cried. By this time they were settled in Florida, yet we visited a lot back and forth. I had a small apartment in the inn that they could use when they were in town. Dad went to a couple of AA meetings in Hancock with me and liked them. This was no surprise given his lineage and his parents' abuse of alcohol.

In the back of my mind, I had planned to stay sober for one year and then see if I could drink. My resentment over my marriage was unresolved. I was angry because the man Roxanne was dating had been my first sponsor in A.A. Once again, I felt betrayed and abandoned. My response was obvious—all that I needed was an opportunity. This attitude was like *me* taking poison and hoping that *you* die. I had been a "vengeance drinker," so why change now?

I was on a vacation in the Dominican Republic with the newest and best-est girlfriend. We were seated outside at a nice restaurant in Puerto Plata, and I was fantasizing away all my problems in this romantic interlude. The waiter brought wine. She drank, and when he asked me if I wanted wine I said yes, because I really did! I decided to have a glass of wine there and then. I vividly remember the tartness of the red wine and the feeling I felt as I swallowed this fruit of the vine. It was mixed and conflicted. AA really screws up your drinking. I now know that my desire to feel "normal" and please this woman were major influences, triggers to my addiction, yet underneath there were much deeper conflicts that justified my drinking. The scary part was that nothing much happened. I only had that glass of wine, and another day in paradise continued on.

When I returned to Hancock from the Dominican Republic, I continually ruminated on my own self-deceit. Drinking was always on my mind, yet unknowingly I was in full rebellion and relapse. I decided to "control drink." For me this would only be the wine coolers that were popular during that time and didn't look like a real drink that contained alcohol. I would not touch my favorites, beer or liquor. I quickly found out that I couldn't just have one or two wine coolers; this did nothing for me. I drank more, and soon was having six or seven and still was not "buzzed." Thoughts and justifications of "kicking it up a notch" were in the back of my mind. If I ever drank socially, it had lost its purpose for me. I knew that if I continued, I would be "all in" with alcohol, and then probably cocaine too, and God knows where that would lead me. ... Or I would not drink again. I was one of the lucky ones who put the drink down for good. My sober date is December 7, 1986.

Chapter 22

SOME CHANGE; THEY FEEL THE HEAT, SOME; THEY SEE THE LIGHT

MAKING DECISIONS WAS ALWAYS A task for me. As an almost-middle child, I had basically relied on watching others' behavior; it was how I learned. I lacked the social skills needed to relate to a peer group or have close friends. Folks with alcoholism, my peer group, did not usually make the best decisions. Learning about recovery from any addiction and actually recovering from an addiction are two distinctly different processes. I had never separated out these processes from each other. The process of recovery is like growing up all over again; maturation is more successful the second time around.

I had ideas about selling the inn and going back to school. I had gone back to AA and spoken about my drinking again. There was not a lot of surprise from my fellows. They simply said, "It happens, move on." My ego, of course, was expecting at the least a large band and welcome-back banner. I went back to meetings outside of the immediate area—Binghamton, Walton, Deposit, and a fledgling group in Hancock that met weekly. I was concerned about relapse and made an appointment with a therapist who would profoundly affect my future; her name was Janet Garbarini. Janet was an expert in mental health and addictions. When I told her that I was concerned about relapsing, attempting to garner some sympathy, she simply said, "You already did." I was instantly in love; I had found my savior, or so I thought.

Therapy was an interesting process. I mainly went to try and impress this gorgeous woman who was my newest fantasy. She was nonplussed, and again and again led me back to the real problems, the cores of my addiction. This depressed me even further. I could not manipulate or control Janet. The answer to my mental state came from an older man who had about twenty-three years of sobriety who was attending an AA meeting in Deposit one Thursday night. I knew who this man was because his daughter helped teach ballet lessons to either Mercedes or Marne at a small studio in Deposit. Talking about depression or any mental health issue was chancy at that time in AA. There were the old-timers who told you what to do, and then there was a growing group of folks in recovery from drugs and alcohol who felt that mental health and addiction may be related. The jury on this issue was still out at that time, and certainly more so in rural meetings. This man spoke about his own struggle with depression and alcoholism. I was sitting there thinking that he was telling *my* story.

Once again, I connected because there was another who had the same bizarre thoughts and feelings that I did. In therapy, we continued to explore my secrets. Secrets are useful, probably essential to the human condition, and I had plenty that I did not even know I had. In recovery terms it's called peeling off the layers of the onion. Janet knew that I was a relationship addict first, very codependent, and my addiction to alcohol and drugs was only a symptom of my needs that had been unfulfilled as a child. I needed to know more about these connections, yet I was afraid what I would actually find out. Was I a sociopath? Would I ever be "normal"? Fuck the drinking and drugging. What was really underneath all the years of self-medication? Had I lived thirty-some years minus a sense of self? In my mind it seemed that as a child, I was a survivor. As an adult, I was a victim of that childhood. Actually, as an adult I became a volunteer at some time. I may have been powerless over alcohol, but I was not choiceless when it came to my behavior. Lesson learned.

Chapter 23

Back across the Bridge

I DECIDED TO PUT THE inn up for sale and coldly found out that there was not the market I had anticipated. Reality check! The hospitality business had changed quite rapidly in a few years' time. Insurance on a four-story wooden building that was one hundred years old was expensive. Taxes were high and profit margins were slim. I focused on the kitchen, cooking and catering, yet I had underestimated the social and the financial consequences that my extramarital affairs and family issues had on the business. Those who knew I had quit drinking would tease me about it or sometimes just plain harass me, wanting me to take a drink to be like they were.

I also underestimated the importance of running a legitimate and welcoming bar business. The history of the personalities behind the bar was rich with local color. The relationship between the bartender and the customer was primary. When you change bartenders, it really matters to the customers. From the beginning I had seen some terrific personalities behind the "stick," as we called tending bar: Charlie Rock, Elton Clark, Charlie Adams, Kris

Karcher, David Schoonmaker, my brother Gerry, Gordy Janner, and Stanley Ancewitz. These were all men with big personalities and good people skills. I did not have these traits, and now with my lost interest in alcohol, bar customers lost interest in the inn. I also knew that some of my help were stealing. With this in mind, I redoubled my effort to sell the inn. I had caught two of my employees taking money; buying drinks for tips and not ringing up all the sales and pocketing the extra. I figured it was the price I had to pay for someone else managing my business affairs. I also tolerated this because of my own guilt over how absent I had been as a businessperson.

I had acquired a delicatessen, The Pickle Barrel, for a very reasonable price. I let my present girlfriend manage the business. She was somewhat withdrawn and finally told me that she did not like my daughters, Mercedes and Marne, which was a major conflict for me. It turned out that she had plenty of other conflicts too. I was surprised when I found out she had another apartment and was planning on leaving me to hook up with Marne's godfather. What goes around does come around! Today, unlike then, I can't blame him. She was gorgeous, could hit a golf ball a mile, and was a local gal. I thought we could have a life together. We separated, and after some attempts to keep the deli going at a profit, I had little confidence in its ability to make money. There were unpaid bills and rent, and McDonald's came to town. I sold it cheap. In the end, I lost money but learned a lot about trust on that deal.

I needed to learn about this "thing" called addiction—and from folks I didn't know and who did not know me. I needed to grow up again. There were a thousand questions I wanted answered, and I needed more than I was getting from AA meetings. Once again I attended Sullivan County Community College and parlayed the courses from my other degrees into an AAS degree in drug abuse and alcoholism counseling. Instead of drink, I was becoming addicted to healthier habits: college, exercise, and parenting being job one. I had less interest in the business. Instead, I wanted to be a successful student, and for that I needed to study. It is amazing what I accomplished when I didn't spend my day behind the "neon curtain."

I managed to sell the inn right before I sold the deli. I didn't get much for it—about $225,000. After subtracting all my debts and Roxanne's share, there wasn't much left. One of the smarter moves I made was to enroll at the Maywood College School of Social Work. It wasn't just my idea. My therapist had gone there and I followed her example. The smart part for me was that I paid the tuition costs before I pissed away any of the money I made selling the inn. I did some stupid stuff too, like overinvesting in renovating a house on Fall Brook Road. It was a manic move, and I "had" to do it. Again, the need to "fix" things drove me. I was able to recoup some of the money when I sold the Fall Brook property, yet I still miss the place to this day. I also bought twenty aspirin vending machines and attempted to start a vending route in Binghamton—the biggest waste of ten grand ever, really dumb.

The good news though, overwhelmingly, was that I was busy. I was taking care of Mercedes and Marne, I was in graduate school full-time, and I had a full-time job at Daytop Village in Parksville, New York. There was a lot of traveling to and from school in Scranton, Pennsylvania, then from home to work. This gave me plenty of time to work out my thoughts and feelings without substances. I listened to recovery tapes in the car and classical music—a lot of music.

At this time, my dad had been diagnosed with lung cancer, and it was inoperable. While on his deathbed, he asked me what I was going to do now that the inn was sold. He had always been my closest support, and we became close friends after I stopped drinking. I said I was not sure yet, but his response floored me:

"Why don't you do whatever you want to do?" he asked. "What a revelation," I wanted to say back to him. "Why didn't you tell me that twenty years ago?" But I already knew the answer; I would not have listened.

Chapter 24

THE FLAT EARTH SOCIETY

ONE OF THE PROGRAMS I was involved in when I worked at Daytop Village was a state department–funded training program. I was part of a team that went to several countries to train health-care professionals in the treatment of addiction and mental health. I was intrigued by this program and flattered that I had been chosen to represent the mental-health department for Daytop.

I first traveled to Pakistan where we were to work in their old capital, Lahore. The airport looked as if it had been bombed. There were craters along the runways, the buildings were all in disrepair, and the interiors of the terminal were deep yellow from cigarette smoke. The cab drivers fought over which one of them would carry our bags and drive us to our hotel, as apparently there were few foreign visitors and business was slow. One large man with a deep beard acted as if he was in charge of doling out work. He finally settled the fight among the taxi drivers. We then left the building and headed to a line of about sixty yellow taxis. The cars were various models of Fiat knock-offs, and what we could see looked well worn. The taxi driver knew two words of English, "No problem," and we knew no Farsi.

So there we were, feeling that in some ways the clock had been turned back. On the Pakistani Airlines flight there from Amsterdam, we discovered that some airlines let passengers smoke, and that cloth diapers were still used in other parts of the world and were often left under the seats or in the bathrooms to cure. Another clue that we had crossed a culture line was that the females on the airplane were dressed in Western garb when they got on the plane, but were dressed in traditional Pakistani dress when they got off. It appeared that most of the folks other than us had transportation waiting for them. We were not so lucky. When the fighting broke out at the airport over our transportation to the hotel, I knew we were in for something special.

As we approached the taxi, the driver signaled for us to wait a while a few feet from the vehicle as he rousted a sleeping man from the small backseat. I found out later that the drivers rent out the backseat for some of the guys who worked other shifts to live in for some extra income. The man got out and quickly went away; however, on his way out he pointed to one of the tires that was flat, mostly on the bottom. "No problem" said the driver as he hurried to get the spare out of the front passenger seat. Soon he had changed one bald spare for one bald right rear tire, and he signaled us to get in. Apparently the boarder had no access to soap and water, because the body odor in the car was gag level. We rode to downtown Lahore with our heads out the windows to avoid asphyxiation. We were taken to a Holiday Inn that was smaller and less ornate than the ones stateside, yet appeared newly built. After the usual check-in hubbub and passport examination, we each had a room. The first night, I was surprised by the call to prayer, but I was curious more that anxious. The muezzin calls folks to prayer five times a day. Each of our rooms had a prayer rug and an arrow on the dresser that pointed toward Mecca. Religious prayer was a part of everyday life for most of the folks there.

We had a driver with a jeep who worked for the American Embassy in Lahore. He picked us up the next day and drove us to a larger and very ornate hotel to meet the rest of our team. We would move there, since it seemed that the Holiday Inn was a mistake in the itinerary. This hotel was magnificent. The floors were all hand-laid pieces of cut wood in various mosaic patterns. The Indo-Paki food, especially the beef, was the best I had ever tasted. Each night a man came and took our shoes to shine; he left them outside our room for the next days' wear.

The training went well since most of the "students" were grateful to be attending. Most of the females had more education than the average male; they also wanted out of the country. These young women explained to us that they lacked young men who were suitable for marriage, and they wanted to leave the country to find husbands. Most of these women were trained nurses, doctors, and social workers. A feminist movement was brewing there according to one social worker I talked with. The movement was quite conservative by our standards. Instead of independence, these women simply wanted the opportunity to have a marriage, children, and a job. It was heartening to work there, and I hope to return someday. One of the saddest parts of our stay was seeing the poverty of the children, many who lived on the street. It was very difficult seeing a child carrying a baby and begging for a handout. The problem was that when you gave to one child, multitudes appeared from everywhere, one looking worse than the next.

Other movements were going on there too. When we visited the crowded areas of the city market in Lahore, I noticed that our driver was staying close to us. He confessed that he was also our bodyguard, and he showed us an older Colt .45 automatic under his long "chemise" that most men wore over baggy pants.

Apparently even at that time there was concern about foreigners, especially Americans, agitating for change within their political system. This guy told us that he was pledged to keep us safe, and that he was a lieutenant in the Pakistani Army assigned and paid by the American Embassy. He was the kind of guy you wanted on your side.

From Pakistan, we flew to China where we met with a nationally honored psychiatrist named Dr. Wan. Dr. Wan had been trained in London and Moscow and spoke English well. We had simultaneous translation when we worked, and two assigned females who taught at Yunnan University who spoke English and guided us around during our free time. One of the guides was Chen Lei, who during our non-training time showed us around the city of Dali where we were staying. Dali is in Yunnan province near the border with Myanmar. There was a new city that was a free-trade zone and looked like any small American city, and there was Old Dali that was built centuries ago and had a wall surrounding the town. The food there was different but fresh and wholesome. Our students had many questions about the USA and how we lived. Many of the children wanted to come up to us and touch us, as they had not seen anyone different than themselves except the hill tribes that lived in Yunnan. I got a haircut on the street, and the wife of the barber brought me dinner afterward. I sat and ate with them and their children in their small shop. Even though we did not speak the other's language, we all seemed to enjoy each others company.

This area of China is part of the famous golden triangle where heroin poppies are grown and processed in neighboring Myanmar. Those caught smuggling heroin into China, at that time, had one chance for rehabilitation. They spent a year in a type of boot camp, learning to change their behaviors. If they were caught smuggling again, they were beheaded. There was a low tolerance for smuggling drugs there.

Other places I went were Thailand, Malaysia, Peru, and Brazil. The common denominator during the eighties in all of these countries was the addiction to alcohol, heroin, and tobacco. There was also a rapidly growing problem with HIV that was spread through the use of shared needles by addicts, unsafe sex, and prostitution by both men and women.

In Brazil, the children of the streets huffed glue. It was mixed with cocoa powder, which I assumed made it more tolerable. They would put the glue in a long plastic bag and run the bag up the sleeve of a long-sleeved shirt. The end of the bag was folded over through their hand so they could just put the hand to their face to huff. You could tell these kids easily because they walked like zombies, only half in control of their bodies. There were also kids who sold candy for a living and a place to stay. Usually an adult would have a house where they could have a room that took the money from the candy sales in exchange. Most of these kids were about five or six years of age.

While in Thailand, we worked with folks who ran the adolescent jails. Child gangs basically ran these adolescent and teen prisons; there was little opportunity for rehabilitation. Drug use and addiction was rampant. We helped the Thais develop a "therapeutic community" system for the adolescent jails that became a model for the incarcerated youth in Bangkok. Most of these kids wanted a safe and rehabilitative environment. I found the Thai people very open to change, and they adapted to their surroundings quickly. Success always feels good, and it feeds one's desire to do more.

In Peru, a similar problem with managing adolescent prison populations was even more difficult. While we were there, some of the students we were training who worked at the prison were caught in a riot and some were stabbed and beaten. We stood little chance of helping with a recovery model there. There were deeply rooted cultural issues that had their beginnings in slavery and skin color hierarchy. These caste systems flourished in the closed society of a large prison system that was a city unto itself.

When we were in Brazil, we lived in an old monastery in the mountains outside of Sao Paulo where retired clergy could come and live. Our teaching model was to set up a mock therapeutic community and practice the various roles that residents would have in a real therapeutic setting. Our rooms were sparse, and it was cold at night in the mountains. We were fed local farm food like raw milk and homemade yogurt. The attendees were very warm and loving. While there, I had a spiritual experience that opened me up to a different way of thinking. I had a dream about a statue of a saint that stood in the front yard—I believe it was St. Anthony. In the dream, I was washing the statue with a scrub brush and soapy water. When I woke up early the next morning, I went and got a bucket and a brush and washed the statue. A dream is something I would not usually take literally, yet in this case, I could not stop from getting up early and washing the statue. One of the brothers who lived there told me that the day I washed the statue was the saint's birthday. I felt useful, alive and whole. It was one of those special moments that probably are around all the time and I had ignored them. In recovery, we refer to these moments as a "God shot."

Chapter 25

Growing Up, Again

Attending graduate school full-time, year-round in a sixty-four-credit clinical social work program was no joke. I was not used to attending anything for two years without a break. I felt entitled after selling the inn, and somewhat lazy. Really I was burned out and needed quiet time away in a safe place. Marywood College, in Scranton, Pennsylvania, was a great place for me to transition to a new life and a change of careers. It was small enough to feel comfortable, yet large enough to have diversity.

I felt insecure in some classes; many of my "issues" with relationships factored in. Most of the professors were women and so were the students. We were encouraged to get to know our fellow students and learn from each other. Many of the courses focused on human development—the growth of individuals and their mental health needs. Little was taught about addictions, although, I believe that at least two of the professors I had were in recovery. Some of the students had difficulty seeing alcoholism or addiction as a mental health issue. I found this to be a major shortcoming in most social work programs. Many of the students wanted to avoid addiction issues and focus on mental health or community social work.

Daytop is a therapeutic community that began treating folks in the late fifties and sixties for heroin addiction. Prior to that, heroin and marijuana were mainly drugs found in the entertainment business and in minority areas of the city (black). When addiction became a mainstream issue (white), in the late fifties, public awareness grew and therapeutic communities became the treatment of choice in New York City. Daytop Village was the brainchild of Monsignor O'Brien, then a priest, who had a parish in upper Manhattan. He started the first Daytop Village residence on Staten Island, New York. Daytop Village eventually became one of the largest providers in the world for the treatment of addicts. Their story is worth reading about. What a great guy the monsignor is, the salt of the earth.

At Daytop I began to succeed. First I was an alcoholism counselor at the Parksville facility, and then in the eighties I was an HIV pre- and post-test counselor there as an internship for my Marywood Social Work program. After graduate school, I did some training for Daytop with their aspiring counselors. I was promoted to the Supervisor of Mental Health Services for the Daytop facilities in Sullivan County.

At Daytop Village we had students from Thailand, including a psychiatrist who had come to stay here for one year as an internship. I invited them to Marywood to see the school and to talk to one of my classes about their experiences. We later went out to dinner with the professor to a local Thai restaurant. I wanted to share what I was learning at school and at my work with others because I needed validation for the direction I was going in. Some of the longer papers that I wrote for the more difficult classes got very high grades and compliments from the professors. I was surprised that I could actually complete the degree and do well at it; my GPA was around 3.67 when I graduated. It took two full years and about $30,000, but was worth every cent. In the end, it was therapeutic as well as academic. From that point on, I knew that my happiness would come from helping others, and that my vocation would be some form or other of human services.

My business acumen nagged at me; it really had never left completely. For a brief time, I opened a psychotherapy and counseling private practice in Hancock, but it was not a business success. Folks there were either too healthy or they remembered me too well. However, I was able to help a couple of folks and two families that had sought counseling. In the end, I had a few clients and learned a lot about private practice psychotherapy and its true purpose for me. It was definitely not the business part that counted. There were many professional options open to me at this time, yet I had made a commitment to help others and needed to do that and stop my grandiose thinking. My brain chemistry was readjusting to a normative way of processing my thoughts and feelings, yet the original anxiety and fear about success remained. "Once a pickle, never a cucumber again."

At my home in Fall Brook, I spent many days by myself with an old tractor and cart. I went into the woods and picked rocks from what were the remnants of old foundations of time and people passed. Perhaps they were working farms at one time. I built stone walls around the house and the driveway. I see now that I was practicing building boundaries, one of the essentials to good relationships. I gardened, built a pond, raised chickens, and had two old plug horses for my girls to ride. Mercedes loved it; Marne couldn't have cared less about the horses. In many ways, those years alone with the girls pushed them beyond their childhood years; we grew up together. Mercedes could drive the tractor and the car and shoot a handgun when she was only fourteen. Marne was four years younger, and like me, she was shy. Marne liked being carried as a young child; she needed that closeness. Mercedes liked her independence and privacy, and Marne liked me taking her with me wherever I went. Mercedes grew to be somewhat rebellious; Marne liked being closer to family. This came as no surprise since I had been active in my addiction the first four years of Mercedes's life. They both really wanted their dad and mom together like most kids from divorced parents.

I wanted to remain in Wayne County after selling the house on Fall Brook Road. I also knew that I was too isolated in Fall Brook. Snowslides and mudslides and icy roads were challenging my ability to get the kids to school on time and to get myself home after work. I bought a house with a barn and twenty acres in Shehawken, Pennsylvania, not far from my father's childhood farmstead on Hickory Hill. I do not know what drew me there, but it seemed like I belonged there at that time. I thought I was so differentiated from my family while growing up, yet I relived many of those experiences in my recovery.

One example proved I was reliving my past life from the Lake Como farm. I built fences, had a huge garden, put hay in the mow, and kept three horses. I raised pigs and chickens. The girls named the pigs, Bacon and Eggs. My problem was I wanted to do it all in a hurry. I re-sided my house with shakes and little help from others. I did have a lot of help from a Kubota tractor with a bucket that I used as a scaffold. The garage was in bad shape, so I put on a new roof and added two full bays with a concrete floor. I rebuilt the inside of the barn and made horse stalls. Sometimes it was just not possible to do some things by myself, so I hired a carpenter to teach me how to do the many things I couldn't do. I had some chickens and some rabbits that I accidentally killed with rat poison. I should have known better than to put rat poison where the smaller animals could get at it.

The attic of the house in Shehawken was infested with bats, and the barn was full of crap when I moved there. The prior owner had made a dump out of the creek bed below the barn. He later moved and built a house on a pond that creek ran into. What goes around continues. He and I had been friends, yet the promises made by him about the house and what was supposed to be completed by him did not get done. There were the bats that he never removed, and I had to take all the junk out of the barn. I took down a chicken coop that had rats coming to it and found an old saddle blanket buried in the mud. Since we had horses, I figured it a good find and I had it cleaned. Unfortunately, the neighbor came and took it one day when I was not there.

I should have said a lot to him about the way he treated me. I lost respect for him over time for several reasons, although I did want his friendship. My self-esteem was growing and I had less energy for folks who wanted to use me. The last I heard, he and his wife were sailing the world. One thing he was brilliant at was his ability to build things; he could conceptualize how something looked and build it. Paul also was a crack mechanic and fairly good at auto bodywork. We shared some important moments in sobriety together since he was a member of the fellowship too, last I knew.

To keep out the cold, I cut firewood to be used in the wood stove in the living room and the wood-burning furnace. The warmth and fragrance of burning hardwoods filled the house through the winter and into the spring like only they can. I put new windows in the house. In the early spring, I planted herb gardens and replaced the front porch and built a laundry room. I sanded old floors and pulled out carpet and remodeled the upstairs bathroom. Then I built a riding ring to train the horses in. At the end of all the work, I too went broke like my dad did on our farm in Lake Como. Nothing that I did was frivolous, and all the work was a learning experience. Someone got a deal. I hope whoever they are, they like it there.

My great-aunt, Lillian Curtis, lived in the house I was raised in at Preston Park. I was able to see her weekly and listen to some of the history of the family. Lillian was the last person I could talk to about the family history. We would sit in the living room, and as she spoke, I would relive my childhood in Preston Park. Funny how when you grow older, things look smaller.

The ride each day to Daytop for work and the trip to school in Scranton logged about five hundred miles per week, and the pressure of having the majority of the responsibility for my two daughters kept me stressed. Terry Kulikowski, the girls' grandmother, was a saint who never judged my separation or divorce from her daughter. She was always there to help with the girls. Sicorro Marin, whose husband is in the fellowship, helped by taking the girls after school until I could get home from work. Jackie Ramburg, a single parent herself at the time, helped me get through some of the "female" stuff with my daughters. These are just some of the folks who helped me parent Mercedes and Marne. Yet, no matter what the situation, when I crossed the bridge each evening into Wayne County, Pennsylvania, it felt like home.

I married again in September of 1993. My wife, Sandy, was working as a nurse and attending graduate school to become a nurse practitioner. At that time, we had the majority of responsibility for my daughters. Mercedes was not adjusting well to our marriage and was a typical pain-in-the-ass teenager. In many ways she felt displaced again, and although she attended counseling, her behavior was directed at Sandy and me. I made excuses for her bad behavior many times out of guilt. She can tell her own story someday! Marne was young enough to bond with Sandy, and they are close friends to this day. Sandy and I had two children together,

Katie-Rose and Liam. They were born in Binghamton—Katie in 1995 and Liam in 1997.

After graduate school, I was offered a job teaching general psychology at Sullivan County Community College. My egotistical self wanted the status of teaching college courses. At the same time, I worked part-time for Daytop as a social worker. After one year, Sullivan County cut funding for the program and the college let me go. I was angry, and some of my old habits of resenting people who disagreed with me returned. I had put the professor who recruited me on a pedestal. When he fell off, so did I. I was fortunate to return to Daytop full-time. One more lesson in right-sizing myself.

I was adjusting to working for others now, something I had not really ever done before. Being accountable and following direction was not a cakewalk for me. This was especially true around nuances and politics in and of the work setting. When I owned the inn, I answered to no one else (or so I thought). Finding the appropriate social and professional boundaries was experimental for me during this period. What I really needed was a dose of humility.

Chapter 26

BACK TO THE FUTURE

SANDY AND I SPENT ONE year living in Middletown, New York, renting a townhouse with our new family. Mercedes was off to college in Stroudsburg, Pennsylvania, and Marne was to finish middle school while staying at her mother's house in Hancock. Marne would then come to live with Sandy, Katie, Liam, and me. Sandy was offered a good job in Newark, New Jersey, as a family nurse practitioner, while I was working in New York City part of the time and in Sullivan County part of the time. Again, I had been promoted to the directorship of the mental health division for most of Daytop Village. I had responsibilities in about eight different facilities all over New York state, and the excitement of the job was its own reward. Working in New York City is a unique experience. I highly recommend that everyone try it for a time; it changes one's perceptions about what people can tolerate.

We moved to Clifton, New Jersey, and rented for a year from a creep. It was a two-family house, and a single mother lived upstairs with a young child. The landlord constantly harassed both of us. When she left, the landlord stole her deposit. When we left, he tried the same tactic. I had enough esteem to take him to court. In the end, we got most of our money back.

Clifton is an older city sandwiched between Passaic and Patterson. Rents were high and my credit was shot. I borrowed some money from my brother Michael and talked a lady up the street who had a house for sale into selling it to us at a fair price. Given the circumstances, we had a fairly roomy house and back lawn. The area of Clifton around our house was rough. While Katie and Liam benefited from a great elementary school and after-school programming at the Boys and Girls club, their future for middle school was limited. Marne excelled at the high school and was involved with theater and musicals. She adjusted better than the rest of us. She also made good friends with a small group of gals and guys who hung together and were all college bound. Part of the benefits of living near New York City is that many ethnicities were represented in our neighborhood. In the evening on my walk home from the train or bus, I could smell the many different types of cooking in the air. What a different and varied world I had entered. Diversity does not happen by osmosis.

I had taken a leap of faith and declared bankruptcy. This was a legal step I had never considered I would do; I was much too prideful. Being sober from alcohol does not make you money wise. I always had money in my pocket when I was in the inn. Money was security. I could buy friends, drinks for the crowd, toys for my girlfriends, and lack of accountability for myself. After having a few years sobriety, I began to see that I had always been living in fear—fear of what others thought about me, fear of friendship, fear of my feelings, and most of all, fear of failure. If I had a pocketful of money, I could keep the fears at bay. Alcohol was a sideshow, a red herring. Alcoholism was the result of not facing my fears. Now I had failed financially, and in many ways I was not as afraid as I thought I was. Most of the fear I had was what fear is, unreal. One advantage that I had now was that I was sober. Also my tendency to watch and learn that I learned as a child became an asset. There is a lot to watch in New York City.

I continued to go to AA and NA meetings. Clifton, New Jersey, had some great twelve-step meetings, especially a men's meeting on Sunday morning. It was here that I met Barry, who became my best friend, AA sponsor, attorney, and biking partner. We logged over three thousand miles each year riding for hours on weekends. Often we went on seventy-five-mile rides around northern New Jersey and up Route 9 from the George Washington Bridge to Nyack and back. We rode year-round and often as snow fell.

Sometime in 2000 I left Daytop. They were a great place to grow up, but I was again like a young man who outgrows his family and needs to leave for other opportunities. I went to work for Liberty Management, a for-profit company that hired me to run an outpatient substance abuse clinic in Kew Gardens, Queens, New York. The commute was long, sometimes an hour on trains alone, yet the pay was more than I made before, and I needed to do a better job financially with my present family. The company was focused on one thing: money. I spent the year trying to justify the company's mission while they bounced petty cash checks and seemed only concerned with their profit and not the success of the clients.

When my supervisor, Joe, who had his office in Manhattan, left the company to work for the State of New York, I started looking for a better job, closer to home. I found one with Corporate Counseling Associates. They offered me a job after the first interview. It seemed that co-occurring treatment for the combination of addiction to drugs and alcohol and mental health issues was finally becoming important. Sometimes timing and luck are good friends. After I was sober, everyone seemed nicer and my luck improved!

I went to work for Corporate Counseling, which is a private, upscale Employee Assistance Program (EAP) that had some very large and potent customers throughout New York City, New Jersey, and Connecticut. Their offices were on Park Avenue South and Thirty-Second Street. This business was new to me. In addition, I was working with a highly professional group of peers and some of the best therapists I had ever met. A perk of the job was that I could use my office for a private psychotherapy practice after hours. In New York City, where office space was expensive, this was a nice bonus. There I was able to build a practice and secondary income. The hours were long but rewarding. Every clinician looks forward to having a private practice. It is autonomous, and we can work with the tools that suit the client best. If you don't try to make a living at it solo, it usually is a good supplemental income. Now I seemed happy. I had a great job, my commute was tolerable, I worked for this great company on Park Avenue and Thirty-Second. We were on one of the upper floors with a panoramic view of Manhattan, facing south from our staff lounge. What more could I want? This was August of 2001.

Chapter 27

September 11, 2001

PENN STATION IN THE MORNING is always filled with a large herd of human beings vying for the escalators that go up to the street during "commuter time." It is the opposite in the evening at quitting time. We all seem to hold our breath like we are underwater and exhale at once when we reach the top as if the air is cleaner on the street. On that day, the sky was that deep blue that we get on the east coast during the fall. The air was still and rich with oxygen, and there was not a speck of cloud in the sky. Heading east toward my office, I fell in with the hordes of folks.

I was on the east side of Broadway when I first heard and

then looked up seconds later to see a jetliner flying very low down the avenue, maybe less than a few hundred feet up. *Very strange,* I thought, but it is New York City and maybe there was some newly discovered airspace rule that was in effect in that area. I also thought that it could be a plane needing to land at Newark Airport, which is south of Manhattan. At least he would have three major airports plus private Teeterboro Airport to choose from if he needed to land. As I reached our building, I ran into Bruce, one of the administrators, in the elevator. As we went up, I asked him if he had seen that plane and he said, "Yeah, looked odd. Wasn't it flying too low?"

I came up to our floor (for some reason I think we were on the thirty-fourth) and walked into the staff area to drop off my lunch. Someone said that a plane had hit one of the Twin Towers. We all looked south to see that one of the towers had smoke coming out of it. Neither Bruce nor I put the low-flying jetliner and the attack on the towers together yet.

If you had ever been to the Twin Towers, you knew how massive they were and realized that they, in effect, were a city of their own. Visitors from out of town came there as tourists, folks got married there, and people from all over New York shopped in the mall there. Six people had died when the towers were attacked in 1993 by terrorists with a bomb hidden in a truck underneath the towers.

I had been to various seminars and trainings in Tower 1 on a high floor where New York State had offices, and once I had brunch in the restaurant called Windows on the World on the top floor of that tower. We generally agreed that whatever had happened, the fire department would put out the fire and someone would explain how a plane could have strayed that close to such a massive structure. Someone commented that a small plane had once hit the Empire State Building and not much happened, except to the pilot. We were all thinking "small private plane."

Then we all watched in horror as the second plane, a large jetliner, hit the second tower. Everyone looked at each other. Someone got a television and set it up in the lounge. Within minutes, we knew this was no accident and that people were probably killed when the planes hit the buildings. There were no details at that time about a plane hitting the Pentagon and about an errant airliner somewhere in Pennsylvania. The images of the planes crashing into the towers are a picture now etched in American minds forever.

In our office, reactions were strange, as everyone reacted to this trauma in different ways. Jose, one of the supervisors, seemed numb. I said to my supervisor, Debra Presti, "Would you sign off on this paperwork so I can go back to work?" My defense was to ignore what was going on and bury myself in work, or if food was available, to eat. The lounge was filled with employees who seemed like they were in "slow-motion." Several folks from New York City were crying, but my relationship to New York and the towers was different from those who lived in Manhattan and nearby Jersey City. It would become complicated as the days unfolded.

In denial, we watched the towers burn. It appeared as if the fires grew larger and there was more and more smoke coming out of the windows. No one dared say what was on his or her mind—which was that the buildings could or would fall down. We watched, stunned and in disbelief, from our safe perch high above Park Avenue as the two giants tumbled one after the other. Clouds of smoke and dust were the only things visible as Tower 2 crashed and then later, Tower 1 fell to the ground.

Corporate Counseling, where I was working at that time, was a small yet dynamic group of about twenty clinicians and ten or so account managers. The managers were also clinicians, but they handled client company relations while the other clinicians, like myself, handled individuals, families, and couples who sought consultation and therapy through their EAP programs. One of our client companies was the Port Authority of New York and New Jersey. These are the folks who owned the buildings or were in the process of buying the towers from the owner Silverstein Properties when Al-Qaeda attacked. The medical department was, I believe, on the seventy-second floor of Tower 1, and all were evacuated. Seventy-seven others who worked for the Port Authority died that day. Corporate Counseling also had Empire Blue Cross and Blue Shield as clients in the towers, and they lost eight folks. Phone cell service that used an antenna on Tower 1 was knocked out completely. The realty of being able to connect with loved ones from on the ground could not happen.

By early afternoon, there was silence on Park Avenue and in many other parts of Manhattan as survivors and others seeking exit from the city headed north, east, and west out of the city. Folks who were covered with dirt, white dust, and debris, and others who were dressed in clean Brooks Brothers suits walked side by side quietly. The Brooklyn Bridge was full with folks walking east out of Manhattan; any ferries across the Hudson River to New Jersey going west were packed. The George Washington Bridge was closed, as there were rumors that it may be attacked next. Others headed to the Bronx. The ripple effect was evident as the horror spread out away from ground zero into the other areas of Manhattan and other boroughs. People were courteous; no one honked their horns. Manhattan was stunned, numb, and quiet. At about 3:30, I headed toward Penn Station because some trains were now beginning to run under the river to New Jersey. I hitched a ride on one of the small "Spanish" buses that ran back and forth to New Jersey, since the Lincoln Tunnel and the GW Bridge were closed. They were taking people to Penn Station. Usually this trip cost $3; that day, just crosstown was $20, but I didn't complain.

Within days, the Port Authority medical team was operating at full capacity in Jersey City at their security center. I was asked to go there for most of the week to offer counseling and trauma therapy to survivors and the significant others of those killed. While most therapists have a different view of trauma-based disorders today, at that time the model was based on folks "telling their stories" to an empathetic counselor or group. This was done in an attempt to normalize some of the inordinate thoughts that folks create around their fear and repression of the traumatic event. I learned much more about the malady of trauma as I listened to the folks who were in the towers when large jetliners loaded with jet fuel crashed through the structures. They redefined my expectations of what I thought I would hear. This went on for weeks as bodies were uncovered, usually in parts, and those body parts were slowly identified.

One young woman I remember and still think about from time to time had immigrated to this country, completed a college education, and became employed by the Port Authority. She worked in Tower 1. She then married a young man who was a first responder (EMT), and they had just bought their first home together and were planning a family. Her husband came from Queens to the city to help in any way he could, as so many first responders did. This included police, firemen, and emergency medical techs. By a miracle, this woman survived when Tower 1 came down. Two friends near her perished in the implosion as a blast of air threw her out of the way of falling debris. Her husband, an EMT, came to the towers to find her as well as help others. He went in and she came out; his remains were discovered some weeks later. She was severely traumatized. I saw her often for over a year. Her emotional state did not improve very much initially.

Another story that remains with me today is that of a trip with a chaplain and a captain to a fireman's home in the Bronx to inform a young mother with a baby and an eight-year-old son that the searchers had finally found her husband, and his dad, dead in the rubble. Actually they found his torso. I will never forget the boy's face as the hope of Daddy coming home to him drained from his eyes when he was told that his dad was dead. All this time between the attacks and the identification of body parts, this young boy believed that his father would be found alive.

One elder man talked to me about his son who was an engineer and had worked on the construction of the buildings. He refused to believe that his son had perished. He told me the story over and over again about how his son knew the building thoroughly and that he would have found a safe place to survive and be found alive. That did not happen.

For the next four years, I was assigned to the Port Authority and provided counseling and therapy to these folks and others with related issues. I worked with two great doctors: the medical director, Dr. Duke, and his associate, Dr. Fisher. The managers, Lillian, Robin, and Karen, and a nurse, Nadine, were all very affected by the event. Their important work kept them from feeling at times. Nadine entered into an abusive relationship soon after the attacks and passed away from heart disease. Her heart was broken in many ways; certainly her guilt about surviving the attacks while others perished was part of it. Nurses and other staff had just escaped death, and these folks were entirely committed to helping others while they, too, were suffering. It was a privilege to work there.

Most loss is often the end result of an expectation. We all get older and eventually die; folks accept the loss and move on. It's more difficult when children die before their parents, because it is not expected. The expectation is that parents die first. When the unexpected happens on such a large scale, we experience a *reality leap*. On 9/11/2001, *reality leaped* ahead of normal expectations as never before in America, especially in New York, Washington, and Pennsylvania. America was stunned. We could not get our thoughts and our feelings around the reality of what just happened. Being attacked, having over three thousand folks sent to fiery deaths ahead of their time was unrealistic to us; we were in shock as a nation.

Another aspect of this trauma to contend with was that over two hundred people either were blown out of the building by the explosion of jet fuel, or in some cases they jumped. The concept of jumping from a building this large to a certain death is difficult to get one's head around. I cannot imagine jumping from eighty stories up. Firemen were crushed in the building as it fell down. People were burned alive in collapsed elevators and stairwells. These images remain anchored in many folks' minds long after they watched, unbelieving, as the attacks unfolded. I can only imagine what images remain in the minds of survivors.

Clearing the towers' footprint and searching through the rubble after the initial search for survivors went on for weeks. News organizations repeatedly showed the planes hitting the buildings. Some amateur films were made of the attacks and the ensuing calamity and were shown on TV over and over. The splat of people hitting the ground after jumping or falling from the floors above the hit line could be heard in the background. It was a scene you could not look at or look away from.

When the Port Authority moved its main medical facility back to Manhattan, on the East Side, many of the employees could not come back or would not come back to work in the city. This required desensitization for several clients and took time and repetitive small steps toward success. Many left the Port and went on to other jobs nearer home. One man of Indian descent was afraid to come into the city from New Jersey where he lived. This was a case of acute traumatic response that required baby steps if he was to be successful at returning to his job. Also, I believe that he was afraid of being seen as "an Arab," and he feared being harassed or worse at that time.

After a couple of attempted rides into New York City from New Jersey, on the Path Train with me, he couldn't handle it. As an option, he said that he would try to have his friends drive him in on a weekend when the city was less busy and when he had the support of his family and friends. The friend who was driving got lost after he crossed the George Washington Bridge that Saturday and ended up going the wrong way on a one-way street. As his luck would have it, there was a cop car parked on the street, and the police saw these darker-skinned Indian folks in a car in an area that they would not usually be, driving the opposite way the street allowed. They were stopped, and one cop made them get out of the car and be searched, while the other cop was checking out their IDs, etc., on the radio. Obviously anything that could go wrong and interfere with this guy's anxiety reduction did. He never went back to the Port to work, and we stopped seeing each other.

There were countless cases of heroism and countless cases of less-than-up-front behavior that followed this tragedy. Rumors had it that the firemen who found the large Tiffany safe in the rubble now were wearing gold Rolex watches, and that retiring policemen took advantage of overtime duty to boost their paychecks before retirement as their benefit was calculated on a percentage of their last year's salary. There are also many men and women who dug in the dirt as unpaid volunteers for weeks. These earnest folks ingested the fine dust from the sheet-rock that was pulverized by the explosion of jet fuel and the collapse of the buildings. Many of these people later became sick from the toxic air they breathed. I believe that the then-governor of New Jersey paid a visit to the site and declared the air safe to breathe (so much for trusting her).

I attended the annual memorial services for the next three years; each time they became more political. What didn't change was the impact of the reading of the names of the people who died there that day. The children of the dead will someday have their own stories of this time and place when America was attacked.

Chapter 28

Moving, to the Left Coast

Like many people who lived in and around New York City, I soon became aware that many everyday occurrences would never be the same again. I was now referring to a still, blue cloudless day as a "9/11 day." Crossing Broadway, I found myself looking up. What did not help were the silly color-coded warnings that perpetrated fear and mongering for a phony war that came from the federal government during the Bush administration. It did not make me feel safer. In my heart, I knew that our billion(s)-dollar defense industry screwed up, and thousands of civilians paid for it with their lives.

New York became militarized. It was announced that New York City helicopters would be armed with fifty-caliber machine guns, courtesy of homeland insecurity. Entering the Lincoln Tunnel each morning on my way to work was a stark reminder of some soon-to-be-revealed ongoing danger. Policemen with machine guns stood at the entrances to the tunnel; trucks were stopped and searched, and occasionally cars with Middle Eastern–looking guys were stopped so that their occupants could be frisked too. You could see the confused look on their faces. With some commuters, simply having brown skin qualified them for a stop and search. The police were more likely to be there on sunny days, not when it was raining or snowing. I was beginning to become angry at the whole damn city. A great place that had breathed with positive excitement now sweated with negative anxiety. The oppression eventually smothered a city that had always represented freedom with an umbrella of stale, toxic air.

At home in Clifton, I was ten miles removed, but the tension was still with me two years later. I watched as my own neighborhood changed, and I projected this change as being more dangerous. I now noticed Middle Eastern folks more often than I should have, whether on the bus, train, or airplane. I remembered that I had shopped at an Arab-owned (Egyptian) clothing store on Fortieth Street and conjured up thoughts and feelings that these guys knew about the coming attacks. I also felt guilty that I had never said anything about it. This was "secondary trauma" that was manifesting within.

It was around this time that my brother Gerry had left Florida and moved in with my brother Jim in Portland, Oregon. Gerry had a drinking and drug problem, and he needed to exit living with my mother; he was looking for a new start. Gerry had aged rapidly because he could not come to grips with the divorce from his wife and the rejection from his adopted children. His "reorganization in spite of his problem" was not successful. One of the many defense strategies those of us who abuse substances employ when the place we are in at the time gets too hot to handle and we have unresolved emotional issues is that we flee. Gerry soon had a job in Portland with a pipe company and worked hard at the job. His coworkers liked him, not unlike the Gerry of the past.

Gerry also was, unfortunately, diagnosed with prostate cancer at about this time. He opted to have his prostate removed, which was one of the options he was given from his doctors. Soon he had cancer in his lungs and liver; in other words, he was terminally ill. I came to Portland to see him and offer any assistance that I could. We had our differences over his behavior in Florida, yet he was my brother and who was I to judge anyone. Gerry was in the hospital at that time, and it was apparent that he would not live much longer. I saw him again when he was released from St. Vincent's Hospital on hospice care when he was heavily medicated and failing rapidly. His main concern was attempting to take care of us by reassuring us that he was going to get more treatment and would survive. I returned to New Jersey and began making plans to move to the West Coast. When I would do it remained unplanned, yet I was thinking one year would work.

In the next year, I talked about moving with my family. Liam was nine and Katie was eleven. The options for middle school were bleak. Part of this was my paranoia about my kids being the only blond-haired children in the middle school. The housing market was ripe, and selling should have been easy. Neither my wife nor I really understood the depth of duplicity with our real-estate broker. We both just shook hands with the realtor and expected her to work to sell the house. This dragged out, and by luck, our one-year contract with her and her company was up. We relisted the house with another woman, and the property was sold within a month. Again my luck was holding. By this time we had already moved to Battleground, Washington.

Finding a house is easier than finding a home. Prior to moving, we flew out to the Portland area and looked, and looked, and looked. In the city of Portland, what we wanted or expected as acceptable was priced out of our range. There would be one nice house next to a crappy one, and the schools did not generally have a great reputation either, which added to our frustration. I found a house that was two years old that had been listed with the broker we had worked with when we were out in Portland, shopping. The house was in the town of Battleground, Washington. The elementary and middle schools were walking distance from our house, there was no renovation needed as in the prior houses I had owned, and the town had enough population (sixteen thousand) to provide a choice in groceries and shopping. The housing market remained high, and we overpaid for our house as many others have recently discovered.

The better news was that I had been in touch with a rehabilitation start-up in Vancouver, Washington, about twelve miles away. Here rush hour is just about one hour, and the commute was easy. I was given the opportunity to build a rehabilitation center program that had been started in a new community building in Vancouver. The exciting part was that my years of experience in human services and rehabilitative work were now paying off. As the clinical director, I started with a sixteen-bed detoxification unit, a sixty-bed drug and alcohol rehab unit, court programs designed as alternatives to incarceration, an ACT (outpatient) program, an adult outpatient drug and alcohol unit, a mental health outpatient program, and several other smaller programs. The best thing is that they were all under one roof in a new building with other community service providers in the building.

When I began, we had about 35 employees, and when I left almost five years later, the organization had about 150 folks working there. Over the years that I was there, I felt that most of the work had been done to make the organization a credible entity, and it was. Unfortunately, the CEO was probably the least talented and least motivated person I had ever met. She continued to take on contracts from the county and state that we lost money on. I had seen this coming for at least two years and turned one of the sixteen-bed units that had been an inpatient facility for the Deaf and Hard of Hearing (that was publicly funded and bleeding money) into a private-pay rehabilitation "co-occurring" unit that at that time saved the agency's solvency. Recently, a psychologist whom I worked with described the organization as a "slow sinking ship" after my leaving. Another thing I learned in recovery: "I am responsible for the effort, not the results."

When I left New York City, I had a thriving private practice in addition to my job. I attempted to re-create the same in Vancouver. This was somewhat successful; however, my job was very busy and I could not handle the same number of clients. If you want to be a private therapist, do it in a big city, where folks want therapy before they need it, and they have the resources to pay out of pocket.

Today I am the administrator of a sixteen-bed mental health short-term crisis program in Portland, Oregon. Residents stay for an average of six days to be stabilized and return to their home setting, and often their supportive outpatient provider. Some live in group homes, some in their own homes, and some in shelters; sometimes some live on the street. It's rewarding work, and the company I work for is a major player in residential treatment for the persistently mentally ill population in several states. I still go to AA meetings and support recovery with service to my home group and my men's group. I honestly believe that each part of my life so far has been in preparation for the next; this I can take no credit for.

When I look back on the evolution of recovery from the first trauma, there is no doubt that children who are traumatized have many needs that often go unmet. Addiction is simply a coping mechanism to live with the trauma. Addiction is a dependency born of a habit that has gone awry. There were many children that I grew up with that endured trauma, and some who did not survive. One of my best friends growing up and in my adulthood was J. R. The loss of his leg in a stupid accident changed his life forever. Eventually there were not enough horses to bet on or drinks to have. At the cusp of his recovery, he ended his own life. Given his potential as a young man, he could have achieved any level of accomplishment he desired. I miss him.

When children are traumatized, they cannot speak to anyone about their fears. Often the person they trust the most is available to them the least. Looking at my formative years as a teenager and a young man, I was just plain lucky and had an angel on my shoulder. David, Victor, James, Billy B, BillyL, and numerous others died prematurely, often drunk, looking for relief and wanting to feel normal. I would guess that they, like myself, grew up with what I call a "hole in the soul." No amount of food, sex, money, booze or drugs, or fast motor vehicles, and no amount of power or the illusion of control, could fill that hole. Not only does our brain respond to trauma with chemical changes, but it also accommodates addiction. But that's for another book. Thanks for reading.

Postscript: In a few years I will move back to the area where I grew up, at least for the summers. I miss the Delaware River, the surrounding woodlands, and my friends who are still there. I also dearly miss my grandchildren, who live in Wayne County, Pennsylvania. Oddly enough, I do not miss the inn.